MOVING AROUND

Cobbled street, Rovinj, Croatia

MOVING AROUND
A Lifetime of Wandering

Michael Webb

goff
BOOKS

Stone Circle, Avebury, in the English west country

Serpentine Pavilion by Toyo Ito, re-erected at Beaulieu in the South of France

CONTENTS

Armani billboard, Milan

Post office staircase, Pula, Croatia

FOREWORD

This is a compendium of incidents, observations, and discoveries on travels around the world. I've drawn on memories, journals, articles, and correspondence, arranging the notes in a rough chronology and by location. Some are composites, of repeated trips to favorite cities and countries over many years.

Early expeditions were loosely structured and serendipitous. As a film programmer in the 1970s, I would take a few days off from screenings in exotic locales to look around. I've spent the past four decades writing architectural books and articles, planning every journey in detail to explore a diversity of buildings and meet their authors. So the tone shifts, and there are digressions on film, design, and art along the way.

Even the shortest journey can bring rewards, and I've been a compulsive wanderer from the time I could walk. In this quirky travel memoir, I've recalled some of the places and people that seized my attention, but have omitted many more. There seemed no point in adding to the voluminous coverage of famous buildings, so (with a few exceptions) I've stayed off the beaten path, especially in such familiar locations as London, Paris, and Rome. I hope these recollections and images may prompt readers to make their own discoveries and share my nostalgia for what has been lost. — M.W.

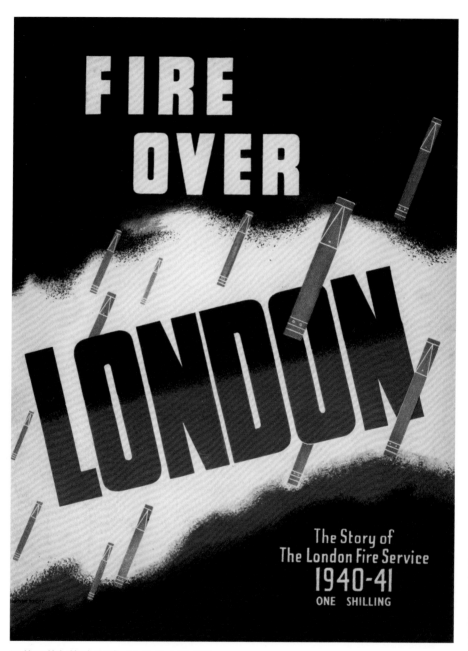

FIRE OVER LONDON

The Story of The London Fire Service 1940-41

ONE SHILLING

Booklet published by the London County Council in 1941

VIOLENT BEGINNINGS

My earliest memory—real or imagined—features the London blitz. At age three, I was snatched from my cot and carried to a shelter my father had constructed in our garden while on leave from the Royal Air Force. The sky was illuminated with searchlights playing off barrage balloons, and the menacing hum of enemy bombers was accompanied by an explosive chorus of flak. Or so I was told afterwards, and the image has become as vivid as a scene from a war movie.

My father was off giving orders in some undisclosed location, so my mother resolved to take me out of harm's way and chose the south-coast resort of Worthing. She loved the theater, and may have remembered *The Importance of Being Earnest*. Whatever her reason, it was a poor choice, putting us on the flight path of our side and the enemy. The next four years were full of action: stray bombs and exploding mines, alternating with crashing aircraft (theirs and ours), and occasional strafing by a stray Messerschmidt. I took all this as a normal way of life and doubt I was traumatized by the noise and breaking glass, though there were nights when I got little sleep. My chief interests at that time were watching the aerial armadas passing overhead and collecting. Keys were my passion. Imagine my delight to find a row of US tanks parked in our street in preparation for the D-Day landings. The trusting Yanks had left the keys in the ignition and I took them all.

The reckoning came quickly. At school assembly, the headmaster asked the culprit to identify himself. Red-faced, I confessed. I had sabotaged the war effort, and elsewhere in Europe my parents and I would have been shot. Instead I was locked up for a few hours in the police station and released with a warning. I would like to think the experience inoculated me against a life of crime and I hope the tank drivers weren't put in the brig. [1940–44]

AN INNOCENT ABROAD

At age 14 I fell in love with Leslie Caron after a screening of *An American in Paris*. Ignoring the end title—"Made in Hollywood, USA"—I believed I would find her dancing on the quais and persuaded my parents to let me join a school trip to the City of Light. That wasn't easy. My father may not have believed that "wogs begin at Calais" (as many of his countrymen then did and--as Brexit showed--still do) but he harbored deep suspicions of foreigners. I won him over, and my anticipation was increased by the master in charge of the excursion permitting us to have a taste of wine. No question that Leslie, when found, would succumb to the sophistication of "un vin blanc, s'il vous plait."

The poster that took me to Paris

The trip fell short of expectations. England was a poor country back then, and our spending allowance was meager. It rained as steadily as it did at home. We trudged through the puddles and lodged in a pension with damp sheets. There's an image by Henri Cartier-Bresson of a French school group, in regulation capes and berets, clustered atop a tower of Notre Dame in that same year. As a collector of period French photography, I cherish that image, but the experience of being there didn't thrill me at all. Paris was a sodden slog and Leslie was nowhere to be found. [1951]

⋆ ⋆ ⋆

The following summer, I fell in love with France. I had been corresponding with Jacques, a boy of my own age, son of the police chief in Alençon. He invited me to stay with his family, and again I took the ferry across the English Channel. I remember little of that month except that no one spoke a word of English. My French improved exponentially and it came in useful when Jacques's uncle asked me how to make Scotch whisky. I had only the vaguest idea but I improvised freely. I only hope he didn't take my recipe literally.

A moment of glory came soon after, when Jacques and I went fishing and, with beginner's luck, I landed a large pike. We carried it home and a feast was organized for family and friends, with the *brochet* as the centerpiece. Artichokes were served just as the power failed and I had to eat this strange object in total darkness. Afterwards a drop of Calvados was poured into my empty coffee cup and I realized the dream I had first had in Paris of becoming a man of the world.

Flash forward 50 years and I was back in Paris for a month, researching a book. Leslie Caron responded to a proof of *Through the Windows of Paris*, with a lovely tribute: "At last a clever book with so many precious addresses! The French are inventive, tasteful and individualistic. I go to many of those shops myself—treasures!" Maybe one day I *will* meet her. [1952]

PLAYING ROUGH

Taking a degree at the London School of Economics was not my choice. My headmaster—an Oxford man—advised against it. "I wouldn't mind if they were honestly red in their politics," he said, "it's pink I object to." My father was paying and he insisted, hoping I would learn the ways of business and support him in his retirement years. I was lucky to have as my tutor Michael Oakshott, a conservative in the tradition of Edmund Burke, who had succeeded Harold Laski, chief advisor to the Labor Party. Pink had turned to deep blue, and I received a sympathetic hearing when I told him I had no aptitude for figures. "Switch to medieval political thought," he advised. "It's a useless subject but it will give you three years to discover what you really want to do."

Oakshott was as much a misfit at LSE as was I. The year before his appointment he had been arrested for indecent exposure – sunbathing nude on a remote beach. Two old ladies perceived a pink blur, went closer and decided they were shocked. He defended himself and secured acquittal on the grounds that his accusers were motivated by prurient curiosity. His inaugural lecture proclaimed that "We sail a boundless and bottomless sea," relying on good seamanship to stay afloat. The faculty understood that he was repudiating the state planning they held dear. Learned journals were about to review his *Guide to the Classics* when they discovered he meant classic horse races, not Horace and Virgil.

His wise counsel liberated me from futile study. I took that opportunity to act, produce a revival of Monteverdi's first opera, *Orfeo*, and direct several plays. Every summer the drama society went on tour, inflicting its meager talents on unsuspecting foreigners, and I inherited the task of leading the invasion. The play had to have universal appeal and plenty of roles. In a moment of madness, I chose *The Three Estates*, a 16th-century morality in Scottish dialect that had been rediscovered and acclaimed at the Edinburgh Festival. Virtues and vices contended for the soul of Everyman, and the symbolism would come across even if the dialogue was unintelligible. Or so I thought.

We traveled in a vintage bus and our goal was Greece. Two of our company were well-connected Athenians and they assured us that theater of Epidaurus (seating 14,000) eagerly awaited our coming. Our first engagement was more modest: a Catholic girls school in Austria. Until that moment I hadn't realized that the play, a product of the Reformation, was violently anti-Papist. The nuns noticed immediately and there was no invitation to stay over. We headed into Yugoslavia, where the bus broke down and had to be towed by oxen to the nearest garage. Patched together, it careened down passes into Greece, the brakes barely functioning, but we had to waste several days in Salonika recovering from food poisoning. Epidaurus was scratched from our schedule. We chugged across the Pelopponese to Patras, where our second and final performance was staged in an open-air cinema, competing with a much-amplified showing of *Bus Stop* in another alfresco auditorium. Given the choice between Marilyn Monroe and a scrawny pack of English students mouthing Scots, the Greeks voted with their feet.

The final act of the drama played out in a field near Foggia. We were as broke as the bus and all but three of us hitched home. Drawing on the Italian I had learned while staying with a family in Pavia, and the expertise that had won me an economics degree I negotiated a sale of the bus to local fishermen. The modest yield allowed us to travel back by train to London where we discovered that we had illegally exported the vehicle and would have to buy it back, transport it home, or have it destroyed. Happily, the fishermen had already stripped it of everything useful and were willing, for a small consideration, to push the shell over a cliff in the presence of the carabiniere. [1956–59]

Parthenon at sunset

GREECE

Byzantine church at Mistra

Nine months later, I was back in Greece, and that first solo trip is still a succession of vivid tableaux. I traveled alone, by local bus and boat, with the *Blue Guide* but no set itinerary, finding hotels and company as I went. In retrospect it seems like a dream, for the tourist tide had yet to break. The few foreign travelers were welcome guests, prized for their novelty.

I climbed up to the Acropolis after a downpour had emptied the site, sat on the steps of the Parthenon feeling the warmth of the marble, and returned after dining on the roof of a taverna in the Plaka. As the moon rose above Hymettus, the ruin seemed to quiver with life, bleached white in the darkness. On the slope below, in the theater of Herodes Atticus, a chorus rehearsed a classical drama, the shadowy figures moving slowly in intricate patterns, their song faintly echoing.

At the port of Piraeus the next day I missed the morning boat to Hydra and, on impulse, took the next, discovering on board that it was bound for the island of Aegina. "Mounts will be found in readiness," advised the *Guide*, and there at the quay were two donkeys. My case was strapped to one, I clung to the other, and we climbed to the deserted ruin of a temple that rose from a carpet of wild thyme. From Athens I headed south through the province of Arcadia to the abandoned city of Mistra, where I clambered over the hills in search of tiny Byzantine churches. Then to Mycenae to explore the Bronze Age tombs and, like the archeologists who excavated the ruins, I stayed at the Belle Hélène guesthouse, chatting to the waiters, Agamemnon and Orestes.

On an overnight voyage across the Aegean, I slept on deck amid wizened islanders and their animals. Many of them disembarked at small islands, where the rituals of daily life played out on the waterfront to a cacophony of shouts and the slapping of octopus on the stones. I was the only stranger to get off the boat at Rhodes and three touts vied for my custom. A balding man trumped his rivals with a breathless pitch: "Nice hotel it will cost you only 35 drachmae nearest of all to the sea my car will take you there immediately. You come?"

On Mykonos, I had an introduction to the patriarch, who had learned a few English phrases in the bar of the Grande Bretagne in Athens, most importantly, "Let's have a drink." As the brandy flowed, he deplored the rich Athenians who were buying property and spoiling the character of his domain. He told me there were five priests on the island, serving 364 churches, plus a 1/20-scale model, built by a sailor who survived a shipwreck. It was known as the *Sacré Chat* for the cat who leapt over this offering.

On the way back to London, I spent a few hours in Corfu. A friendly resident escorted me to the church of St. Spiridon, where I was accorded the privilege of kissing the mummified toes of the saint. The body is exhumed one day a year to bring the island good fortune, and I was just in time to be swept to the head of the queue. My act of piety brought me luck, for I've spent the past six decades making more surprising discoveries. [1960]

* * *

To get an authentic taste of Greece today, one has to stay clear of the celebrated sites and/or go out of season. In December 1983, Stephen Antonakos, a Greek artist living in New York, invited me to introduce an exhibition of his work in Athens. From my hotel window I could see the floodlit Parthenon floating above the city. The next day I braved the crowds scrambling up the hill and found it fenced off with a tangle of wire. More recently, the authorities have decided to reconstruct the ruin, assembling a jigsaw puzzle of fragments with concrete infill. Impossible to imagine this will have the beauty of the sun-bleached ruin. Better they had left what time and the Venetian bombardment spared, and constructed a plaster replica at the airport, perfect in every detail, so that tourists could take their selfies and continue on to the beaches.

Stephen and I flew to Rhodes, where he had installed a neon artwork in an

Ia, Santorini

ancient chapel – a reference to the red lamp that illuminates a Byzantine icon. In December, the beaches are deserted and there are few connecting flights. I had to fly back

Sgraffiti on a house in Pirgi, Chios

to Athens and make separate trips to islands that are only 30 minutes apart by air. Chios claims to be the birthplace of Homer, and has nurtured several shipping dynasties. Their remittances provide all the income the island needs and so it has retained its character. I stayed in what was once the home of Aristotle Onassis's aunt, and spent a day driving the spectacular road that hugs the coast and is guarded by a succession of stone watch towers. Inland, are walled citrus orchards, taverns serving olives, bread, feta, and tomatoes with rough, local wine, and stone villages. A standout is Pirgi, in which every house is covered with *sgraffiti* – black and white designs incised in plaster. There are circular hexes on the underside of balconies, bands of diamonds and other geometric forms, the odd vase of flowers and crudely drawn animals.

On to an island that is barely there. As Lawrence Durrell wrote, "few, if any, good descriptions of Santorini have been written; the reality is so astonishing that prose and poetry, however winged, will forever be forced to limp behind." Half the island was destroyed by a violent eruption and swallowed by the sea around 1450 BC; the resulting tsunami may have ended the Minoan civilization of Crete. An arc of rock embraces the caldera and was badly shaken by another earthquake, in 1956. What remains, and has been restored, has an unearthly beauty.

I explored the hill villages of Emporio and Pyrgos, and the town of Ia at the northern tip, perched high above the water. Each is a three-dimensional complex of white cubes, freshly painted every spring, with intense color accents playing off the red-brown volcanic rock. Steps link the different levels, and steep paths are accessible only to mules. The ascent is punctuated with terraces, where locals put out a chair to knit or smoke and socialize with their neighbors. In Ia, it was blowing a gale, churning the sea and clearing the air, so that every object, near and far, stood out sharply. The blue dome of a church seemed a displaced fragment of sea or sky. The locals were sure that planes would be grounded, marooning me for a week or two. I half hoped that would happen, but—as in *The Odyssey*—the gods had other plans. [1983]

VENICE

A Comet—one of the first commercial jets—whisked me from London to Venice in the middle of the night. In those far-off days airlines still pampered their passengers, and a BEA launch carried us across the lagoon to their terminal, located in a classical kiosk near San Marco. I dropped my bag at the hotel and set off to explore the city. The Piazza was empty, its stillness broken only by distant voices and the murmuring of pigeons on the ledges. In the light of the street lamps it resembled a great ballroom from which the musicians and dancers had fled.

Elizabeth David, my favorite food writer, advised me I should see the fish market at dawn, so I headed off to the Rialto and waited for sunrise. Flared chimneys and the fretted skyline of the Ca' d'Oro were silhouetted against a colorless sky, just as they appear in the paintings of Carpaccio and the Bellinis. The first pale rays illuminated facades and chased shadows down the alleys and side canals. Vegetables were piled atop the stalls – pyramids of red and green, purple and brown. Then the fish: tight white coils of calamari, delicate pink scampi and mullet, threshing eels, and shimmering bass. Barges unloaded fresh supplies, a gondola ferried the first shoppers across the Grand Canal. It was time for breakfast and a nap. [1963]

Rialto fish market, Venice

Years later I had a reservation to stay at the Antica Locanda Montin, a restaurant with two guest rooms above. A storm inundated the rail track from Milan and the train arrived, hours late, at 2 am. No cell phones to alert the receptionist in those days, and when I finally came to my lodgings, tired and hungry, the hour seemed less promising than it had on my first visit to the city. I rang the bell repeatedly, but there was no response. Later, I discovered that the restaurant was closed on Wednesday so the staff could have a day off, and by 10 the night manager assumed the *inglese* had changed his plans and went home.

The rain had stopped, the air was warm. I sat on the doorstep and played the second act of Verdi's *Otello* on my earphones, having enjoyed the opening storm as thunder crashed over the beleaguered train. The play of light off the canal and the crumbling walls was hypnotic. When the music ended, the lapping of wavelets and the occasional splash of an unseen creature diving into the water kept me diverted until 7 am when the receptionist arrived, full of apologies. I wouldn't have missed it for the world, and I was reminded of those two serendipitous experiences a few years ago when I received a review copy of *Venice in Solitude*, a portfolio of nocturnal images by the German photographer Christopher Thomas. And for some equally idealized, tourist-free images of La Serenissima by day, I would recommend *Dream of Venice*, two slim volumes edited by JoAnn Locktov, an American who cares more for her adopted city than the corrupt cabal who profit from its misgovernment. [1984]

*　*　*

My favorite place in Venice is off limits for half the year. As the monumental core of the city is turned into a theme park, and cruise ships overwhelm and erode the landmarks, the Arsenale provides a timeless, tranquil retreat. In contrast to the palaces and churches, the architecture is functional. In its heyday, this was the world's most productive shipyard, producing a galley every day to fight the Turks and protect Venetian trade routes.

Lions guard the entry arch, which used to provide a short-cut for the vaporetto serving the Fondamente Nuovo and the cemetery of San Michele, but the Italian Navy withdrew permission, claiming that this is still a military base, to be defended from intruders. Every May to October, illusion gives way to reality. The side gate opens to admit visitors to the Biennale, art in odd years, architecture in even. Beyond the exhibits is a world of pleasing decay: crumbling brick, rusting machinery, and barely a launch to ripple the basins to the rear.

It would be worth the trek through art of dubious worth just to see the Corderia, a lofty 1,000-foot-long hall where, as the name suggests, ropes were made. The brick columns flake at the touch and there's a pervasive sense of melancholy, always present in Venice, but nowhere more than here. Power ebbed from the city centuries ago, and pleasure took its place: "Where eas'd of fleets, the Adriatic Main / Wafts the smooth eunuch and the enamor'd swain," as Alexander Pope wrote in *The Dunciad*. The greatest surprise lies beyond, where Jacopo Sansovino's docks and warehouses have been skillfully restored, and the austerity yields to gardens and reflections in still water, with a pair of turrets to guard the rear entrance. No wonder the navy is so protective of its preserve. [2010]

Jacopo Sansovino's docks in the Venice Arsenale

SICILIAN SPRING

For many years, Antonioni's *L'Avventura* was my favorite movie, and its portrait of Sicily as an alien land with marvelous monuments—notably the baroque stage-set of Noto—prompted me to explore the island. In contrast to the spare, monochromatic images on screen, I found a place of exuberant life and color, enriched by a succession of invaders but with its own distinctive character.

Puppet theater banner, Palermo

The Mafia still exerted their power, but the only violence I encountered was staged in the Argento puppet theater, which came to life every night near the harbor. Christian knights were the heroes, Moors and Turks the villains, and the narrow lane was hung with painted banners depicting their contests, blood spurting from mortal wounds. As the street darkened the locals gathered, old men taking the wooden benches for a long night of ferocious combat, small boys sitting on the cobbles in front. The puppet master invited me backstage into a gallery crammed with backdrops and figures as high as three feet and weighing 50 pounds. He busied himself mending tin armor. "It broke in a fight – they fight all the time," he murmured sadly, as though he were a mere spectator.

An hour later, a mechanical piano started up and the curtain rose. Knights swaggered on stage, boasting of their prowess to the approving cheers of the audience. The nephew of Charlemagne was challenged by a Saracen and the battle began. More knights, more infidels, one on one, and then one on six. Swords flashed, cries grew louder, heads rolled, and the audience was roused to fury. Men jumped up to cheer a champion and shake a fist at his opponent. Abruptly a drop curtain fell, and we leapt forward centuries to Garibaldi and his redshirts routing French troops. An intermission, with promises of greater wonders to come: giants, dragons, and devils. Time to leave, in a carozza that carried me through an empty, brightly lit Piazza Pretoria to dinner at the Conca d' Oro.

By day, the city is full of marvels, from taxis that are as daring as the puppets, to the glowing mosaics that Norman knights commissioned for their churches and palaces. The Arabs left their mark, and Spanish rulers indulged in an orgy of baroque ornamentation. Most rewarding are the stuccoed oratories of Giacomo Serpotta, a rococo master. Virtues and martyred saints become characters in a *fête champètre* and piety acquires an erotic allure.

Even more frivolous is the Palazzina Cinese, built in La Favorita Park for the exiled King Ferdinand IV of Naples. It's a close relation, in date and style, of the Brighton Pavilion, also built for a pleasure-loving prince during the Napoleonic wars.

Within is a fantasy of silken streamers, exotic birds on traceried pavilions, and a procession of Chinamen ascending a staircase. A dining room is painted with scenes of rustic life and plates are brought up on lifts from the kitchen below, so that servants should not disturb an intimate party. Lord Nelson and his mistress, Emma Hamilton, were frequent visitors, and she is portrayed in rather abandoned poses around the walls of the Pompeian boudoir.

The urban sprawl of Palermo, with its traffic-clogged streets gives way to landscapes of arcadian beauty, carpeted with wildflowers and heavy with the scent of orange and lemon trees. I took an early train into the countryside and walked down a dusty, white path to the Greek temple of Segesta. The bass of cowbells complemented the tinkling of sheep bells and a shepherd boy gave me an impromptu serenade on his pipe before scampering off in pursuit of his flock. A turn in the path revealed a pediment and the whole roofless shell of the temple came into view. Columns of rough, honey-col-

Palazzina Cinese, Palermo

ored stone rise from blocks that retain the bosses used to haul them, as though this were a work in progress rather than a ruin. The sun cast long shadows and the stillness was broken only by the hum of bees, along with an echo of the bells and a solitary tractor. I climbed to an amphitheater, hollowed from a rocky hillside, overlooking the temple and a distant smudge of sea. Greek settlers recreated the world they left behind.[1964]

Greek temple, Segesta

Medicine man in Fez

Three friends joined me on a drive around Morocco in 1966. Most of the French settlers had left 10 years before, tourists were few, and cars even scarcer. For some reason I've long forgotten we rented a Mini (with right hand drive) in Gibralter, took the Gibair ferry to Tangier, and headed as far south as the roads would allow.

The first day, we crossed the Rif Mountains and drove on through fields that were intensely green from the spring rains and scattered with wildflowers. A tree full of storks looked as though it was plumed with white feathers. An unreal glow from the setting sun highlighted robed figures trudging home, flocks of goats, and a donkey almost obscured beneath its load of brushwood. It felt as though we were traveling, not through space, but back in time, encountering a sense of remoteness and mystery. Fez reinforced that impression, for the walled city is closed to wheeled traffic, and the labyrinth of dusty alleys opened onto mosques and madrassas, which provided the only open spaces. In streets that were canopied with reed mats to block the sun, sounds were muted and the light acquired a dappled, watery quality.

We crossed two more ranges on the way south, pausing to admire pastel-colored cubist villages nestling in the rocks. Urchins emerged from each, intensely curious about these strangers, but curiously reserved. I photographed a group of them and realized they were looking in different directions, having no experience of posing for a camera. We explored the massive stone ruins of Meknès, circumnavigated Casablanca, and discovered the wonders of Marrakesh. Palm groves embraced the ocher walls and the old city was punctuated with lush gardens and architectural gems, set off by the snow-capped peaks of the High Atlas to the south. Slatted metal canopies turned narrow streets into shadowy caves barred with sunlight. Each street is dedicated to a different craft or product, from beaten copper to inlaid wood and embossed leather. In the wool dyers' street, brilliantly colored skeins are looped overhead.

Just outside the walls of Marrakesh, we lingered on the shady paths of the Jacques Majorelle garden, begun by a French painter in the 1920s and soon to become a retreat for Yves St. Laurent. At that time it was still a bit shabby. Cacti, coconut palms, and masses of purple, coral, and crimson bougainvillea played off the buildings, as did the vibrant blue walls and loggias that might have been painted by Yves Klein. The Saadian tombs offered another cool retreat: an exquisite enclave of white marble columns and fretted cedar, incised plaster and colored tiles.

Fez: madrassa

Children in a mountain village

Tumblers in the Djema el Fna, Marrakesh

The supreme spectacle, then as now, was the Djema el Fna, a sprawling expanse of market stalls ringed with cafés and cheap lodgings. In the evening, trading gave place to entertainment. Snake charmers, trick cyclists, and storytellers vied for attention with acrobats who formed dizzying human pyramids, and dark-skinned men dancing to the percussive rhythms of drums and castanets. Almost as fascinating was the multi-racial crowd, wandering from one entertainer to the next with expressions of dazed wonderment.

From Marrakesh we ventured into the desert, passing elaborately patterned mud-brick fortresses and staying overnight in the oasis town of Taroudant. The farthest point, where the road petered out into sandy tracks, was Goulimine. We were lucky to catch the monthly camel market, when the nomadic Blue Men come to town to buy and sell. Early on a May morning, the sun was fierce and the camels seemed distinctly unhappy, snorting and kicking up clouds of dust. The buyers were impassive, scarcely moving and murmuring inaudibly.

Camel market in Goulimine

Heading back, there was a loud crack as we bumped across a dried streambed and we lost a day while the axle was repaired by an ingenious mechanic. That left a little time to explore a few coastal cities. Agadir had been swiftly rebuilt after a devastating earthquake and was a new city of concrete structures designed by local architects in the style of Le Corbusier. From the Portuguese ramparts of Essaouira, bristling with cannon, we continued on to El Jadida and the Gothic cistern in which Orson Welles filmed a key scene of *Othello*. The magic of the trip ended abruptly in the seedy British outpost of Gibralter, where drunken sailors lurched out of bars and pasty-faced expats meandered along traffic-clogged streets. [1966]

Kasbah in Taorirt

GRAND TOUR

US Pavilion at Expo 67, Montreal

The classical world of Greece and Rome lured generations of Brits to sketch ruins, enrich their collections, and enjoy a year or two of study and debauchery. The Grand Tour morphed into the pursuit of pleasure: sunbathing, sailing around the Mediterranean, gambling at Monte Carlo, and partying in beachfront villas. War and austerity interrupted that spree, and a new fantasyland beckoned: the USA. For a century the huddled masses had traveled steerage to the land of opportunity. By the early twenties, mass immigration from Europe had ended, but travelers continued to explore the New World, following in the steps of Alexis de Tocqueville. A college friend whose father was a diplomat in Washington told me of driving cross-country and catching Noel Coward's legendary 1955 performance in Las Vegas at the Desert Inn. American students invited me to stay and provide introductions. However, it was a long way off, one was allowed to spend only 150 pounds abroad, and Europe was a cheap, accessible alternative. Finally I took the bait, stuffed my socks with $20 bills, and flew to Montreal for Expo 67, on to Chicago, and around the US on my own Grand Tour.

Caesar's Palace, Las Vegas

Like Blanche Dubois, I relied on the kindness of strangers. New friends took me to the Fillmore Ballroom in San Francisco and offered reefers to get me in the mood. In Las Vegas—then a straggle of casinos that appeared, like the Emerald City, as a glowing oasis in the desert—I stayed at the Stardust. An American journalist in London had covered the opening of Caesar's Palace the year before, and gave me an introduction to the manager. On the map it appeared to be only two blocks from my hotel so I decided to walk.

Forty minutes later, sweating profusely in suit and tie, I arrived and was escorted to the inner sanctum. I had heard that Vegas was run by the mob, but was unsettled by my first glimpse of power. A hunk of flesh glared across an acre of desk, dark glasses and a scar on the cheek adding a layer of intimidation to a voice that was all bass chords. "Are de boys taking good care of you?" he demanded. "Oh yes, sir, very," I ventured, shivering in the air conditioning. "Good. Because if they ain't, you tell me," he said, a finger jabbing his chest. That was my cue to rise, for dinner and a front row seat at Harry Belafonte's spectacular show. The boys called a taxi to take me back to the Stardust.

In New Orleans, I had my first taste of traditional jazz at Preservation Hall and an earful of conspiracy theories about the Kennedy assassination from an associate of city attorney Jim Garrison. In Texas, I stayed in Athens—which had little resemblance to its namesake—and drove 100 miles with my host in his Cadillac convertible to lunch at Neiman Marcus in Dallas and along Elm Street, following the route of JFK's fatal convoy. My first stop in Washington DC was the President's grave in Arlington Cemetery, a place of inexpressible emotion. And, in those innocent days, I responded appropriately to the white marble memorials with their noble inscriptions. And then to New York, the new Rome, city of skyscrapers and broad avenues, smart guys, and savvy broads.

I had to wait a few days more for that aspect of the city. My host, an anarchist living in the East Village, brought me to an enclave of shabby brick and narrow streets. He showed me the closet where I was to sleep and declared, "Tomorrow we march in Washington to smash the mad bomber." Weakly, I objected; having just come from the capital I was eager to see the Empire State and MoMA. Not a chance. At 6 am we took a bus with other firebrands for the march that Norman Mailer would celebrate in *Armies of the Night*.

The badge of honor on this expedition was to be clubbed or tear gassed. It wasn't my war, and I drifted away to spend much of the day in the tranquil splendor of the National Gallery. Somehow I managed to find the group before the bus returned, and dozed though their boasts of how they had confronted troops with drawn bayonets around the Pentagon. I admired their commitment and felt a twinge of guilt for not having joined them. [1967]

Sunset from the Staten Island Ferry

27

* * *

My second tour of the US was prompted by a Reyner Banham lecture at the Architectural Association. He was researching his book, *Los Angeles: The Architecture of Four Ecologies*, and spoke of the freeways and flatlands, the beaches and the commercial strips. "Where is the real LA?" I asked. "You'll have to go and find it for yourself," he replied.

So I did, flying direct from London and renting a white Mustang at LAX. As I drove up deserted freeways to Pasadena I fell under the same spell as Banham – who said he had learned to drive in order to explore LA as it was meant to be seen, just as earlier scholars learned Italian to read Dante in the original. "Bring me back soon!" I implored an imagined deity, and 10 years later I moved to the City of Angels.

That first trip was full of discoveries, which validated Banham's enthusiasm and his perspective on the place. At that time, I had little interest in Hollywood, but I had already developed a passion for 20th-century design, high and low. I found a city of modernist masterpieces, murals and neon signs, folk art and kitsch – an irresistible combination.

Animated neon sign

John Lautner showed me his latest houses, from the high drama of Silvertop, the Chemosphere, and the Wolf house, to the modest redwood bungalow he built for himself in 1940. Next day I drove to Palm Springs to explore the Elrod House, a flying saucer come to

Edsel emerging from La Puente drive through

"Isle of California" mural

rest on a spur of rock, its circular living room walled in glass and shaded by radiating petals of concrete. I was reminded of that first encounter when I interviewed Lautner for NPR on the morning of the 1994 Northridge earthquake; our talk was repeatedly interrupted by grateful clients phoning to thank the architect for building them a house that had survived the shock.

As impressive as these radical abodes was Watts Towers, the masterpiece of bricolage that an immigrant Neapolitan plasterer created as a work of art over three decades. An elliptical wall, inset with impressions of Sam Rodia's primitive tools, enclosed the skeletal towers, as a ship's hull frames the masts. Every surface was encrusted with colorful fragments of ceramics, glass, and rock, giving the structure a tactile quality and an integrity that defied the city's attempt to pull it down. It still challenges restoration experts. At the opposite pole were the Forest Lawn cemeteries, an obligatory stop for anyone who has wept with laughter reading Evelyn Waugh's *The Loved One*. I found a Disneyland for the dead, a bastion of non-sectarian sanctimony, too refined to be funny. Confronted with an animated Last Supper, the Mystery of Life courtyard and the world's largest stained glass window, I more than ever admired Waugh's genius for satire.

From LA, I drove up the coast road to Big Sur, absorbing the hippie babble over drinks at Nepenthe, and on to the fledgling development of Sea Ranch. Route 128 took me through the hills in a driving rainstorm. It was the perfect introduction to the first cluster of redwood condos and lodges, whose design responded to this wild stretch of California coastline. Waves crashed on the rocks, seagulls wailed, and sea lions groaned, while I was snugly ensconced beside a log fire with my host, estate manager Rob MacLeod. Next morning we rode through the pristine meadows that would later be suburbanized. The idealism that inspired Sea Ranch was short-lived, but I caught it at its peak.

From San Francisco, I flew to Boston and New York to meet architects and see their latest work. Charles Gwathmey had just completed a house and studio for his artist father.

John Lautner's Wolff House

Watts Towers

It was located in Amagansett at the far tip of Long Island, and I drove there on a fine Sunday in September, crawling through traffic on the mis-named expressway. I arrived, hours late, expecting a cool welcome. Instead, Gwathmey Sr. rushed out to greet me and insisted I stay over and drive back the following morning. His son was a modernist in the mold of Corbu, and this early effort was one of the best things he did. House and studio are board-clad Platonic volumes that conduct a dialogue with each other across a meadow.

An introduction to one of President Johnson's aides persuaded me to make a side trip to Washington for a personal, after-hours tour of the White House. Fifty years on, in an era of high security, it seems inconceivable that she could sign me in and take me to the President's private study, the Oval Office (where I sat in his chair), and the Cabinet Room, inspecting the buttons that summoned assistants and ordered Coke, before wandering out to the Rose Garden. I returned, many years later, for the Clintons' dinner to celebrate Renzo Piano's Pritzker Prize, and that was a special occasion, but nothing to compare with my first subversive visit. [1968]

PROMISED LAND

Two month-long trips to the US only increased my desire to live there, so I applied for jobs. Having switched from sedate journalism at *Country Life* to setting up regional theaters for the British Film Institute, I imagined I might find a place in the newly established American Film Institute. Its ambassador to Europe, a raffish ex-diplomat, sought me out and made vague promises. I wrote a letter of application and received no reply. I offered my services as an instructor in film history to several universities; luckily for them and me, the offers were politely declined.

One afternoon the call came. AFI Director George Stevens Jr. phoned to ask if I would care to fly to Washington for a chat. Trying not to sound too eager, I said I'd be happy to do so. "Tonight?" said George. "Certainly," said I. "Great, there's a ticket waiting for you at the Pan Am desk for the 11 pm flight to DC. We'll meet tomorrow." I arrived in the steam bath of a Washington summer, and met with George. AFI had a reserved space in the Kennedy Center, then under construction, and I was asked to suggest some programs. I assumed they wanted a second opinion, having already appointed a program director. I didn't know that he had been fired the previous week, having blown the first year's budget on Milton Glaser graphics. And his dog had wreaked havoc in the office, menacing staff and chewing files. I casually threw out a few ideas and George smiled, "Let's continue this discussion." My hopes rose. "Do I have a job?" I asked. "Of course, why do you think we brought you here?" I suppressed a silent cheer and returned home to pack.

As a movie buff I knew all about trans-Atlantic liners with their spacious staterooms, ballrooms, and siren-filled pools. The *United States*, once the nation's pride, would have failed the audition. She had become a rusty tub and this was to be her last voyage. The cabin was slightly larger than my suitcase, a storm kept pace with us across the ocean, and the entertainment veered to movies I would not have selected for the remotest regional film theater. *If It's Tuesday it Must Be Belgium*, sticks in the memory. There were no sirens and my fellow passengers were green from day two until our arrival in New York in darkness, missing the thrill of seeing the Statue of Liberty. There followed eight years of programming, with frequent trips around the US and abroad, which brought me great delight and a misconceived marriage, which, like an unwatered plant, died from neglect. [1969]

HONEYMOON

Tahiti Beach, San Tropez; Bonnie showing off her tan

Bonnie and I met cute. A smiley Cheshire cat was blazoned across her T-shirt. "Love your pussy," I said, unaware that the word (a harmless diminutive in English) had a different meaning in America. She blushed and giggled, and I was smitten. Knowing that she had run off with her art teacher at Bennington, and probably broken many hearts, I should have held back. But I had just seen Sondheim's *Company*, and was persuaded that I should surrender my freedom as a bachelor. We had great sex, and three months later got married. I planned the honeymoon: to St. Tropez for hedonism, Budapest to select a film program, London to meet my friends.

From the rustic Ferme d'Augustin we cycled to Tahiti Beach, where the days passed in a blur of hot sun, bare breasts, grilled sardines and ratatouille, with lots of rosé before the siesta. We rented a car to drive around the Côte d'Azur, though Bonnie would have been quite happy to stay put until she was tanned to a dark mahogany. In Budapest, she fell sick, and spent several days in bed, sustained by frequent doses of chicken soup (aka Jewish penicillin). She roused herself to meet some handsome young Hungarian actors, but reserved her affections for Miklos Jancso's putsa sheep dog, which resembled a small yak. In London, she shopped: silver from the Portobello Road; Harendt china and Baccarat glass from Harrods. Hospitable friends had us to dinner every night, and we put on a good show, but, flying back to DC, I realized that the chemistry was missing.

It took two years and another trip to Europe before we both admitted that our alliance had no future. She was twice remarried—to a French count and a New York reporter I was told—before settling for her only passion – pekingese. Voltaire got it right: "Plus que je vois d'hommes, plus que j'aime mon chien." Or, as President Truman remarked, "If you want a friend in Washington, get a dog." I should have heeded his advice and her example. [1972]

IRAN

Isfahan: Allavardi Bridge

In 1974 I was invited to serve on the jury of the Children's Film Festival in Tehran. It was organized by Lily Arjmond, a public-spirited friend of the Empress who also established a chain of children's libraries. It took dedication; in poor neighborhoods she was stoned for competing with mullahs who favored pious ignorance over enlightenment. A crisis erupted a few days into the festival when the jury chair, Polish director Jerzy Skolimowski, was caught trying to seduce a high official's wife, and had to make a hurried departure before the code of honor was invoked. I was made chair and got to greet the Empress at the prize-giving ceremony. That was my only brush with royalty until I was seated next to the Queen of Sweden at the Polar Music Awards, many years later. Both encounters were uncomfortably stiff.

The capital was a chaotic mix of reckless drivers, shoddy new buildings, and livestock running free, with a paper-thin veneer of sophistication. The royal palace was an orgy of bad taste. It was a relief to move on to Isfahan, staying at the Shah Abbas Hotel in the old caravanserai fronting the Maidan. For three days I explored gorgeously tiled mosques and palaces, a bazaar with shafts of sunlight piercing the gloom, and the Allavardi Bridge with its vaulted niches. The Friday mosque was a marvel of construction and a masterpiece of ceramic art. At night, the illuminated dome of the madrassa suggested a hot air balloon moored to its minarets.

Yazd: Friday mosque

Isfahan: Friday mosque

Yazd: wind towers draw in breezes

For a brief glimpse of the countryside beyond I rented a taxi and left at 4 am for a three-hour drive into the desert, passing pigeon towers and ruined forts, mud villages, and quanats – shafts that ventilate the subterranean conduits bringing water from the mountains. In the ancient city of Yazd, wind towers catch the desert breezes and draw the air down to be cooled in underground cisterns. I borrowed a hand-drawn street map from the manager of the Air Iran office, and wandered off to explore the maze of narrow lanes in the old quarter. Sand filled the streets and veiled the brightly colored tile work. The Friday mosque had fine 14th-century mosaics, and the custodian allowed me to scramble over the mud domes on the roof and climb one of the two minarets. From here, the dun-colored roofscape merged into the desert, and the modern additions vanished from sight.

Easy to imagine oneself in an outpost of the Foreign Legion, awaiting the assault of a rebellious tribe. [1974]

DEATH IN BUENOS AIRES

Travel around the US was a key ingredient of my job at the AFI. I consulted with museum curators and arts administrators, helping them set up film programs, and haggled with executives in New York and LA, negotiating terms for the titles we wanted to show. Foreign travel was almost as easy and I could justify every expedition by bringing back a supply of exotic movies. I had long wanted to explore South America so I approached the cultural attachés in search of an invitation. The Brazilian, José Neistein, was so excited that he volunteered to be my personal guide. The Argentinian representative was a harder sell. I told him how impressed I was by the renaissance of filmmaking in his country. "Really?" He hadn't heard. No surprise there; it was a well-kept secret. However, he had a job to do, and offered to import some titles in the diplomatic bag. "Why don't I go there and see what they have on the shelf?" I countered. His eyes widened. "You wouldn't mind?" I assured him I would happy to perform this chore.

Checking in at the Aerolineas Argentinas desk at Dulles I was handed a note that read "Don't go." I called the attaché. "Is this an order or a request?" I asked. "I cannot say any more," was the response. My ticket was valid; I had made my plans, and was not to be deterred. Arriving in Buenos Aires I soon understood his concern. A military coup was impending. Isabel Peron and the sinister Lopez Rega were clinging to power and the unions were threatening a general strike. Walls were placarded with Peronista posters – including one in which Juan and Evita look down from heaven on their people. The directors I met had received death threats from right-wing thugs and were planning to flee. A curfew was imposed at 9 pm, just as Porteños were thinking about pre-dinner drinks.

Everything was closed except the cemetery of La Recoleta, a gated community for the rich and well-born. In this surreal city of the dead, streets are lined with family vaults in every known architectural style, from Egyptian and Greek to baroque and art nouveau, even corporate modern with plate glass doors. It's a City Beautiful in miniature. Statuary includes expressive angels gazing skywards, hands reaching down from above, and bathetic renditions of the deceased, slumped on thrones in formal dress suits. Laurel-crowned generals dripping in braid are guarded by stiff-spined hussars, much as pharaohs were entombed with their entourages. There's a nice irony that PAX is the commonest epitaph, for these mustachioed saber-rattlers rarely had to fight.

Professorial busts are propped on a stack of books; a bronze boxer emerges in his robe, looking oddly like a man who has gone to retrieve the Sunday paper from his doorstep and found himself locked out. There are heartrending tributes from the Jockey Club, united in sorrow at the death of a member. A heroic figure, identified as Christ in the guidebook, turns out to be Carlos Pellegrini, founder of the National Bank. Evita made it to her family vault and has become a cult attraction, like Jim Morrison at Père Lachaise, but Juan came from the wrong side of the tracks and was denied admission. [1974]

Evita and Juan Peron gaze down on their fans; La Recoleta cemetery

EXPLORING THE USSR

Fountains at Petrovsk; Lenin's Tomb in Red Square

Invited to the Soviet Union to select a film program, I had the good fortune to be assigned Oxana as my escort. Her father was a general, her mother was a gunner, so no hanky-panky, but she was a charming presence who steered me through the everyday trials and a few that were more challenging. In Leningrad we explored Tsarist palaces and a handful of revolutionary landmarks. Rounding up food and a bottle of wine for a picnic took ingenuity; lacking a corkscrew, I rammed the bottle onto a spiked fence to dislodge the cork, an initiative that endeared me to Oxana.

In Moscow, we took in the usual sights, jumping the long line to glimpse the mummified body of Lenin, and strolling around the Kremlin. But she also allowed me to browse the archives of the Schushev Architecture Museum, where scrapbooks on the leading Constructivists all petered out in 1934, as Stalin enforced the mandate for socialist realism. If only I had known the addresses of the Melnikov House and other monuments of that era I would have asked my KGB driver to give me a tour. Or, I could have bribed a taxi driver with greenbacks. And I might have searched second-hand bookstores for El Lissitsky drawings. Customs would probably have mistaken them for jazzy wrapping paper; only icons were banned from export. What a wasted opportunity!

At that time, the best Soviet films were coming out of Georgia, so a side trip to Tblisi was scheduled. Oxana and I arrived in good time for the 2 pm flight. We waited and waited as she translated successive announcements. "Dear passengers, fog in Moscow is delaying arrivals." (Hard to tell through the dirt-encrusted windows). "Storms in Tblisi are delaying departures." "The plane has arrived and is being cleaned." (A momentary surge of hope). "There are technical difficulties to be resolved." Finally, at 11 pm, "Fog and storms are preventing any more flights this evening." We returned to the Rossia, a 6,000-room caravanserai that was now fully occupied. Oxana demanded that her foreign guest be given a room for the night. Evidently a Westerner outranked members of the Bulgarian Friendship Delegation, so a hung-over comrade was rousted from sleep, and around 1 am I was shown to his bed.

Next day the flight was only two hours late and we fell into the warm embrace of our hosts who—for lack of reliable information—had been camping out at the airport for a full day. They made up for the delay. Shashlik, gutsy red wine, and brandy toasts at every meal.

A succession of remarkable movies introduced by their directors. An excursion to Gori to see the humble birthplace of Stalin, now enclosed in a marble temple. Medallions of the dictator were pasted to every taxi dashboard, like the Madonna that protects Italian drivers. I asked my hosts if they knew their hero had murdered millions. They smiled conspiratorially. "Yes, but most of them were Russians," one responded.

Russian resourcefulness kicked in as the Aeroflot plane arrived in Frankfurt. I had an hour to connect with a Lufthansa flight back to Washington. Our plane sat out on the runway for 45 minutes as though it were being quarantined. Finally we were released and I pleaded with a steward to be allowed to carry my bag to the terminal. The captain intervened, grabbed my case, and commandeered a jeep, driving

Stalin's birthplace in Gori

direct to the Lufthansa plane. There, he persuaded them to let me board by way of the emergency stair, bypassing passport control and the security check. I hugged him in gratitude, marveling at his audacity. [1975]

Church and factory in Moscow

FESTIVAL FOLLIES

You could spend every day of the year at a film festival somewhere in the world, though it might speed you to an early grave. During my ten years as a film programmer, the obligatory stop was Cannes – the largest, most prestigious showcase for art and commerce. The truly dedicated watched six features a day, sometimes skipping from one theater to another in a nearly continuous viewing session. I preferred to limit myself to three, with tennis, a leisurely lunch, and a late dinner to keep me sane. Francis Coppola introducing *Apocalypse Now* was a memorable occasion—a distillation of the brutality and stupidity of the Vietnam War that had recently ended—but the bad far outnumbered the good. Curiously, my strongest memory is sitting in a café on the Croisette, next to a local who was scanning a tabloid. The headline read: "Le Meutrier de Chambéry/a Assasiné son Seul Témoin/la Barmaid Défigurée de Cordes." A perfect opening title for a film noir.

Many festivals had to scramble for the crumbs. LA's Filmex favored inclusivity and it helped to have a sense of humor. An entertaining turkey was *Female Hamlet*. A Turkish director decided it would please an all-male audience to give Shakespeare a contemporary slant, and show the prince as a raven-haired beauty, fetchingly attired in figure-hugging white satin and a scarlet bandana. Polonious is slain with a letter opener; Claudius banishes Hamlet to America with "Rosa" and "Gilda" for escort. "Let's go for a swim while we are waiting for the plane," says Hamlet, and we cut to a beach where the threesome is frisking in string bikinis. Every shot is framed by frantically waving arms and legs elongated by a fisheye lens. How one would have liked to see it at a village movie house in Anatolia. [1976]

A LEGEND REBORN

Abel Gance with film scholar Annette Insdorf

Main Street of Telluride;

My favorite film festival was Telluride, a three-day feast of the new and rare, held over the Labor Day weekend in a remote Colorado settlement. When the mines ran out, it had become a ghost town, but a few trust-funders bought property, and it is now a fashionable ski resort. An archivist, a theater owner and a curator launched the event in 1973, and it was wonderfully informal in the early years. A couple of hundred people would fly in to enjoy tributes to legendary talents, ranging from Gloria Swanson to King Vidor. Movies were screened in the tiny opera house, discussions were held in a mountain meadow, 12,000 feet up by ski lift, and I'd find myself sitting next to Jack Nicholson or Julie Christie, who dropped all pretense in this rustic setting.

In 1979, I met Abel Gance, one of the greatest French directors of the silent era, who had been living in obscurity ever since. A spry 90-year-old, he was enchanted by the invitation – hoping no doubt that he would strike gold in Colorado and realize his blockbuster on Christopher Columbus. He arrived wearing a cowboy hat, kissed every woman in sight, and was given a front-row seat for the screening of *Napoleon*, his masterpiece, which premiered in 1927 as a five-hour epic. Restored to its original length, with a three-screen finale, it was projected outdoors after dark on sheets rigged up by mountaineers.

As the temperature dropped towards zero, the pianist's hands froze and the images unrolled in silence. Fearful of what the cold might do to a frail old man, we persuaded Gance to return to the hotel and watch from an upstairs window. Everyone else huddled under blankets and watched, mesmerized. As Napoleon scaled the Alps, and the image expanded to a three-screen panorama, the moon rose above the Rockies. "Soldiers of France," the Emperor declaimed, "There is Italy. Take it." And the screens turned red, white and blue, lacking only a rousing chorus of the Marseillaise to bring the audience to its feet. A few of us went to congratulate Gance, who was wide-awake and beaming. [1979]

STAR APPEARANCES

A perk of my job at the AFI was escorting directors and stars on stage and entertaining them before and after. Cary Grant arrived at midnight and a seemingly deserted Dulles Airport came to life as desk clerks and cleaners rushed out to stare. I had invited him to introduce a retrospective of his movies but he pleaded a prior engagement – dining at the White House with the President and Queen Elizabeth. Everywhere we went the next morning—to buy a tropical suit and to meet the local press—the reaction was the same: stunned awe. Having started as a straight man in vaudeville and become a Hollywood star almost fifty years before, he confessed it was still agony for him to expose himself.

Leni Riefenstahl had other reasons for staying out of the public eye. Her reputation as Hitler's favorite filmmaker clung to her until her death at age 101, seven decades after she filmed the 1934 Nazi Party Rally at Nuremburg. *Triumph of the Will* may be the most potent documentary ever made and its power is undimished by the passage of time. Her appearance following a screening at the first Telluride Film Festival sparked noisy protests – all the more because she refused to admit that *Triumph* was party propaganda. I wanted to hear her version of the story and invited her to lunch when she was next in Washington. There, and on the ride to the airport, she talked only of the poetry of movement, and how she had orchestrated parades that were unutterably tedious in real time, and cut the speeches to a few sound bites. That shifted the focus to Hitler, who first appears as a savior descending from heaven to be greeted by delirious crowds. Everyone should see the movie to realize the perils of putting blind trust in any god or mortal.

For Charles and Ray Eames I had unbounded admiration and I seized the opportunity to visit their studio in Venice – a former garage transformed into a showcase of past and future projects. A tank of jellyfish and baby octopi recalled the documentary they made to promote the unrealized National Aquarium, and there were models of exhibition pavilions, vintage toys, Indian fabrics, kites, and furniture prototypes filling every shelf. Ray invited me to breakfast at their house in Pacific Palisades and the presentation was a work of art. Back in DC, I invited Charles to introduce a program of his films following the Charles Eliot Norton lectures he was giving at Harvard. AFI had a state-of-art theater but the maestro was taking no chances. He sent a couple of advance men to check every detail and make minute adjustments. That allowed him to saunter on stage in a tweed jacket, tell some good jokes, show his slides of the circus, and know that every image would appear on cue, pin sharp. The short films ranged from *Powers of Ten* to *Sherlock Holmes and the Green Mustache Mystery* – each a tiny gem.

To warm up the audience for the cinematheque I hoped to launch in LA, I invited some of my heroes to present their work. I had met Orson Welles when, years before, I carried a rare print of *Othello* through a blizzard to an SRO screening in Boston. A weekly series of events, *Working with Welles*, reunited associates from the Mercury Theater of the Air, iconoclastic stage productions in New York, and all of his movies. Welles had a standing invitation to participate, and twice he showed up with no advance warning, lumbering onto the stage of the Directors' Guild in Hollywood, hugging old friends, and dominating the conversation. He had perfect recall – and a genius for telling stories, some of which may have been true. Kenneth Tynan recalled a chance meeting in the men's room of the Madrid

Ritz, after which Orson gave him a script and a bottle of brandy, and ordered him to report for duty at 6 am the next day. Only then did he discover that his non-speaking role was to stand with his back to a charge of bulls and look scared. For lack of money, Welles drew on his skill as a magician to secure all the unpaid help he needed to piece together his independent productions, a few scenes at a time.

François Truffaut drew an excited reaction from young women at the Beverly Hills Hotel pool, but he was shielded by his translator, Annette Insdorf. We had a lively chat on stage at the Motion Picture Academy and then flew to Washington for screenings at the Kennedy Center. The morning after our arrival at the Watergate, a blizzard immobilized the city – much to François's delight. Sightseeing expeditions were canceled and he could watch American classics on television all day, interrupted only by journalists who trudged through the snowdrifts to get an interview. He was having such a good time that we persuaded him to stay on for a week and join in a tribute to his hero, Alfred Hitchcock. Annette promised to coach him in English (a language he pretended not to grasp) and he outshone every native speaker at the awards dinner as he declared, "I sink when Monsieur Eechcock put ees camaira on Mont Rooshmoore ..." His teacher glowed with pride. [1972–80]

Painted backdrop for North by Northwest at MGM Studios

THE BEST REMAINING SEATS

When I moved to Los Angeles, I discovered a unique concentration of movie palaces: huge, gorgeously decorated theaters that were built in the boom years of the 1920s. For a decade LA's Broadway was as much the Great White Way as its cousin in New York, but downtown began to decline in the 1930s and the action moved to Hollywood Boulevard. By the 1970s, many of these palaces were shuttered or reduced to showing kung fu triple bills. I persuaded

Ohio Theatre, Columbus, OH

Wayne Ratkovich, a visionary developer, to save the mid-town Wiltern Theater, and rallied public support with *The Best Remaining Seats*, a series of ten classic movies introduced by their stars or directors, most of whom were older than the theaters.

It was a challenging task. We had almost no budget and only a few weeks to clean, repair, and re-light theaters that had been sadly neglected. Happily the projectors were still in working order. Lilian Gish launched the series at the Wiltern, a pink and gold gem of Art Deco ornament within a green terracotta tower. *The Wind*, made in 1928 by Victor Sjöstrom, was filmed in Death Valley, and she described the ordeal of filming in a sandstorm, whipped up by studio fans in the searing heat of summer. The arts editor of the *LA Times* assured me that no one would come to the shows on Broadway – Angelenos knew it was far too dangerous to be on downtown sidewalks after dark. In fact, every performance was SRO and we took the series to the Arlington Theater in Santa Barbara with Mel Oberon hosting, and to Catalina Island, where Douglas Fairbanks Jr. introduced *The Black Pirate*. As *Variety* would have said, the series was boffo, and the LA Conservancy has reprised the concept as a fundraiser over the past four decades.

Lillian Gish was one of the first and greatest film actresses, and at age 87 she could outlast audiences a quarter her age. She still had the porcelain-pretty looks of a silent movie star, but it was spine that carried her through. We went on tour to palaces in Columbus, Milwaukee, and Chicago in mid-winter, and she spent an hour on stage after each showing recalling her years with D.W. Griffith when she had to perform her own stunts. In *Way Down East* she clings to an ice floe in the Connecticut River before being snatched to safety, and the scene still provokes incredulous gasps. [1979]

Dawn at the summit of Mount Haleakala, Maui

ROUND THE WORLD IN 80 DAYS

After 15 years in Britain and the US, film programming lost its allure and a real-estate boom frustrated my attempt to establish a cinematheque in LA. AFI and I amicably parted ways and I was suddenly unemployed. I dreamed of producing a feature and agreed to help José-Luis Borau, a Spanish writer-director, find backing for his script – a contemporary version of *Romeo and Juliet* set on the Mexican frontier. It was coldly received; a similar movie starring Jack Nicholson had just flopped. Job interviews were inconclusive and proposals went unanswered. A friend suggested I use my free time to take a long vacation. Pan Am was offering an 80-day, 12-stop round-the-world flight for only $1,279 and impulsively I bought into the adventure.

Planning a journey can be as rewarding as the experience of travel. I spent a month poring over maps, fantasizing about all the places I had never been, and reading every travel book I could find. Unknown to me, Pan Am was in sharp decline, pruning its routes and patching up decrepit planes. As my list grew longer the options shrank. Finally I had a schedule: Hawaii to southeast Asia, India, Sri Lanka, Nepal, and home, along with the mandated visas and shots. Remembering the hapless William Boot in *Scoop*, who was burdened with a plane-load of excess baggage, I decided to travel light. A few shirts, non-crease pants, and sneakers, plus a lightweight high-tech parka guaranteed to retain or deflect heat, and to be detectable by radar should I stray off course. I packed and set off for LAX on the first leg of my journey.

The departure lounge was full to overflowing, with passengers from the previous night's flight, which had been canceled when a door fell off the plane. They all had reservations; I was flying on stand-by. Two hours passed as the twin loads were fitted into one plane and I

Ceiling of Klungkung Temple, Bali

Bali: Monkey and friend; Barong dance

Bangkok: novices

grew increasingly nervous. Would I be unable to board this and subsequent flights? Might I be stranded at LAX and—ashamed to confront friends—camp out there, bribing departing travelers to send cards in my name from exotic destinations? Twenty minutes to go and my name was called; I had secured the last seat.

The next eleven weeks were as crowded with impressions as the Jules Verne saga, but rather less coherent. In contrast to Phineas Fogg, who took short hops on boats and trains, I was making a few giant leaps. From Honolulu I took a local plane to Maui, rented a car and set off at 4 am to the 10,000-foot summit of Mount Haleakala. Driving up a precipitous road, through rain and fog, I caught occasional glimpses of lights far below, and arrived at the top as the sun rose over the crater's rim. Clouds raced across the sky, casting long shadows as I trekked across the cinders in search of the silversword, a cactus that thrives in this wilderness. Jagged spurs alternated with rounded cones, black silhouettes emerged from the mist, and the larger peak of Mauna Kea rose from the horizon. The Romantics would have called the spectacle sublime.

Bali was earthbound but equally rewarding. Having flown from Hong Kong to Singapore, where I was pampered at the legendary Raffles, I craved authenticity. A bus dropped me in Ubud, then a scatter of farmhouses and artists' studios. I had hoped for a home-stay but the first few I tried were full. As I rested by the road it began to rain and I looked around for help. A man rode up on a motorbike, proposed his brother's house, and carried me off to the Pension Agung.

Half the population bears that name, but this Agung proved an ideal host. I asked him why there was no sign. "This is a simple place," he said, "Rich tourists would find fault." Not me. For $3 B&B I had a thatched cottage in a corner of the family compound. No electricity or running water, so I sat on the terrace, reading by the light of an oil lamp, listening to the hum of family conversation, the chatter of a geko (an insect-eating lizard), and the barking of dogs in the village. Agung's wife served a light supper of nasi goreng and cap cai but, with advance warning, she could prepare smoked duck, sucking pig, and, of all unlikely dishes, shepherd's pie. Next morning, as the sun blazed down on a riot of frangipani and bougainvillea, we breakfasted off fresh-squeezed mango juice, strong black coffee, and banana pancakes.

Back then, tourism on Bali was confined to a few beach resorts south of the airport; only backpackers made it far beyond. My fellow guests included an American sculptor, a Dutch musician, and a French script girl. The islanders still performed ceremonies for themselves

Katmandhu: view from palace

rather than as a paid spectacle. Life was ritualized. Every morning, leaves were set out with a few grains of rice to nourish the gods and be consumed by ants and passing geese. To explore Bali, we clambered onto a bemo, a jitney designed for eight passengers that typically held three times as many, plus livestock and loaded baskets. No springs, bald tires, and, as one traveler observed, you can die three ways in a bemo – from head-on collision, suffocation, or fright. Undeterred by the heat and humidity, we explored temples, swam from black sand beaches, and bought exotic fruits at village markets. On two occasions Agung chartered a bemo to escort us to funerals and festivals, a tooth-filing ceremony (less painful than it sounds) and a nighttime performance of the fantastically costumed Barong dance. Forty years ago, Bali was still an earthly paradise; sadly, mass tourism has put an end to the idyll.

King's birthday parade

I spent a month in India, traveling by train and the occasional plane, from Kerala in the far south to the Golden Temple of Amritsar. Highlights included a day in Jaisalmer, a mirage of fretted towers and Jain temples that rises from the Thar Desert near the border with Pakistan, and another exploring the heroically scaled monuments that Le Corbusier created for the new Punjabi capital of Chandigarh. I splurged on stays in princely palaces – in the lake at Udaipur and, most memorably, in an extravaganza that the Maharajah of Jodhpur commissioned as a make-work project during the Great Depression. For $50 I had a nine-room suite, but the great treat was exploring Art Deco bathrooms by flashlight when the electricity failed.

Bangkok: floating market

The trip was full of surreal moments. Eating serpent soup at a sidewalk restaurant in Bangkok as everyone froze in place to watch the king sweeping by in a white Rolls Royce. Exploring the mysteries of Indian railways, where a tariff board specifies the amount charged for carrying bags of different sizes with top rupee going to the porterage of a dead man. The timetables are pure fiction, though the stationmaster will insist that the trains leave and arrive on time, long after the appointed hour has passed. On overnight routes, you go to the wooden seat you have reserved; bedding is handled by wallahs who materialize as you board, and gracefully accept a tip for this indispensable service.

Nothing topped my stay in Nepal, and particularly the King's 36th birthday parade. At 10 am the parade ground in Kathmandhu was deserted; by 11 the procession was under way, led by mounted cavalry, tribesmen blowing horns, and masked dancers who kept straying off course and being guided back. Everyone from boy scouts to Tibetan refugees and Hare Krishnas followed the vanguard, escorting floats that demonstrated how Nepal had progressed under its benign ruler. One had a row of boots nailed to the tailboard, another bore a suspension bridge and a third displayed a model of a master plan for the city. The ceremony contrasted sharply with the poverty that was everywhere apparent, and I will long remember the waif who shyly begged for alms from a group gazing over the windswept foothills to Mount Everest. As in Iran, I had the sense of standing at the edge of a volcano that was about to boil over. [1979–80]

Protest graffiti in Bharatpur; windblown waif in the Himalayas

NEW YORK WHEN IT SIZZLES

Manhattan: from the roof of the PanAm Building; neon-lit Chrysler spire

Two years after leaving the AFI I was nearly broke. None of my projects had come to fruition and yellowed clippings failed to impress the editors I approached for assignments. A book on neon, a documentary on movie palaces, and a Smithsonian exhibition on Hollywood were still under discussion. I was compelled to share my apartment and pay off my taxes in installments. Annette came to my rescue, naming me her replacement for a summer gig at the 92nd Street Y in New York. By living frugally, I could save most of the fee.

I was to introduce celebrities and interview them on stage after the screening of their favorite film. We kicked off with Robert Redford, a near neighbor of the Y, and *All the President's Men*, which he co-produced, having won the trust of Woodward and Bernstein. Only in New York could an institution pull in so many starry names from the neighborhood, including former mayor John Lindsey discussing *The Last Hurrah*, and Telford Taylor reviewing *Judgement at Nuremberg*.

Days were spent meeting friends, publishers, producers, and museum directors, exploring the city, and photographing neon for my book. To shoot the newly restored lights on the spire of the Chrysler building I was allowed onto the roof of the Pan Am Building – once a heliport. It was blowing a gale and I clung to the rail with one hand, trying to steady my tripod with the other, and hoping I would not be blown over the edge as a helicopter once was. Never has the city appeared more alluring, every light sharp-etched and the bridges like loops of pearls on black velvet.

How I saved any money is a mystery; my friends must have been very generous. Accommodations were the challenge. It was a hot July and the Pullman apartment in Yorkville that I was renting for a song had no air conditioning. Never have I spent so many sleepless nights, but the trip proved hugely productive, restoring my confidence and launching a cluster of projects. [1982]

45

Sidi Bou Said, Tunisia

ARAB ADVENTURES

Film programming proved a hard habit to break. I missed the trips to exotic destinations and watching movies no other American had seen, so I proposed an Arab film series and called on my network of Washington contacts to arrange visits to half a dozen countries in the Fertile Crescent. Ina Ginsburg, an engaging socialite on the AFI Board joined me, and off we flew to Morocco, Tunisia and Egypt, Syria and Algeria, where we viewed films of mind-numbing mediocrity and discussed our program at interminable length with US Embassy staff and local officials. I was itching to get away, and finally the chance came in Damascus, where a taxi driver agreed to take us on a whirlwind tour of the country.

Aleppo Citadel, Syria

We skirted Hama, which had been blasted apart to dislodge the Muslim Brotherhood just the year before, and decided it would be unwise to explore the ruins, detouring instead to Krak des Chevaliers, grandest of the Crusader fortresses. Two thousand knights were quartered within its sheer walls, surveying a panorama of terraced hillsides and the mountains of Lebanon. T.E. Lawrence described it as the perfect castle. On to Aleppo to explore the Citadel, whose walls enclose a rocky outcrop, and an intricate network of souks. Immured in these dimly lit galleries, each devoted to a single trade, I felt as though I was slipping back in time, far removed from the chaotic traffic of the streets beyond.

That impression was reinforced next day in the Umayad Mosque, whose minaret dates back to the early years of Islam, and the courtyarded houses of the Armenian quarter. Still more compelling were the honey-toned ruins of Palmyra. Colonnades and roofless temples rise from the sand, guarded by a hilltop fort, the magic enhanced by the silence of the desert and the absence of other visitors. I longed to revisit these sites at leisure, strolling through shady streets and sun-bleached stones at my own pace, but it was not to be. How much remains from the battles that consumed this legacy?

I had one more unrepeatable experience in the Sahara, flying south from Algiers. Within the Mzab rift valley are five settlements, established in the 12th century by a heretical sect that shunned outsiders. They clung to old customs and interbred, producing strangely shaped heads and cross-eyes. Men were robed and turbanned, women revealed a single eye and brightly colored socks from beneath their burkas. They seemed incurious about the stranger in their midst, as though I was invisible or another order of creation. One old man fixed me with a terrifying glare. "Français?" he demanded. Remembering the violence of the liberation struggle, I realized that was not a good option, but made a worse choice. "Americain," I admitted. "Juif!" he spat, turning away in disgust. I was lucky not to be knifed. Next time, I'll pretend I'm a Kiwi – nobody hates them.

Aside from the airport, a couple of taxis and a dingy guest house, Mzab was off the radar. I walked a mile along the dusty road to Ghardaia, a pyramidal cluster of houses that ascended to a sand-colored mosque with a bent minaret. This might serve as a hook, allowing Allah—in

Roman ruins of Palmyra, Syria

his own good time—to hoist the town and its pious inhabitants up to heaven. Walls were washed in pale tones of blue, pink, ochre, and green, and supported by arches and flying buttresses. Narrow passages encircled the town at different levels, linked by steps, as though a single building had been split into tiers. Small boys darted out, shouted "bonjour," and vanished into hidden doorways. I climbed to the top, removed my shoes and entered the mosque – a bare carpeted room with sunlight filtering in through the sand-encrusted skylight. From there I walked past gardens and saints' tombs to two other towns and took a bus to Beni Isquen, a holy city barred to infidels, though the marketplace beyond the walls surges with life. As the moon rose and lights came on in the watchtowers the magic intensified. [1983–84]

Ghardaia, a walled town in the Mzab Valley, Algeria

ISRAEL CLOSE-UP

Jerusalem: Temple Mount

My introduction to Israel came at LAX, where El Al security staff gave me the third degree, even though I had a personal invitation from the Minister of Tourism. It continued on the flight to Jerusalem where black hats blocked the aisle while praying or arguing about their seat assignments, and I was kept awake by howling babies. On an earlier trip from London I had stayed at the American Colony, a storied hotel run by a Palestinian family, where non-observant Jews can enjoy eggs and bacon for breakfast. This time I was lodged in the Mishekenot Sha'ananim, the official government guesthouse, which was built in 1860 by Sir Moses Montefiore, a British philanthropist, as an almshouse for poor Jewish settlers.

From my room I looked out to the city walls. In 1917, when General Allenby took Jerusalem from the Ottoman Turks, he followed the advice of the British War Office, which cabled him this message: "Strongly suggest dismounting at gate. German Emperor rode in and the saying went round, 'A better man than he walked.' Advantages of contrast will be obvious."

Ada Karmi-Melamede, an architect of formidable authority who designed the new Supreme Court, showed me around, barging into the Chief Justice's office as though she were one of his colleagues. It was the best new building in the city, though that isn't saying much; Jerusalem is a palimpsest of past eras, and new construction pales beside the legacy. Moshe Safdie has struggled to make a useful contribution, and is best known for his children's memorial at Yad Vashem, the most heartbreaking remembrance of the Holocaust I've ever experienced.

Jerusalem: Damascus Gate

Jerusalem: Moslem and (right) Jewish quarters

Weizmann House, Rehovet

In 1967, after the old city had been liberated from Jordanian occupation, Safdie converted a ruined house overlooking the Western Wall, adding airy rooms for his family to the Crusader foundations. His wife, Michal, piloted Moshe Dayan's helicopter during her military service, and she was photographing the Western Wall for a book, brushing off the wild-eyed fanatics who tried to block her path. One of her images shows Jews praying at the base of the wall, Moslems on the Temple Mount above, each unaware of the other's presence. The highlight of my stay was an interview with Teddy Kolleck, the former mayor of Jerusalem, in his office at the Israel Museum. We talked about his career and his struggle to bring peace to a bitterly divided city. Midway though he asked, to my great surprise, "You seem to know a lot about it. Are you Jewish?" I had to admit I was not, but I took his remark as a compliment.

Gideon Shor, a former farmer and veteran of three wars, drove me around the country, from the Golan Heights, where we found graduates of UC Davis making excellent Chardonnay, to Eilat on the Red Sea, where went scuba diving on a coral reef and fraternized with dolphins. We made the customary stops and several discoveries: the former Imperial Airways terminal on Lake Gallilee where flying boats touched down on their way to India (the restaurant was still in operation), and the Ein Harod Kibbutz art museum, built in the first year of independence, which inspired Renzo Piano's Menil Museum in Houston. We toured the house that Erich Mendelsohn built in 1937 for Chaim Weizmann, revered as the first president of Israel. From an overlook near Eilat I could see Jordan, Egypt, and a distant glimpse of Saudi Arabia – a reminder of how tightly Israel is hemmed in by its neighbors. I paid $10 to plant an acacia in a bird sanctuary—an avian gas station that fuels a billion birds en route from Siberia and South Africa—and wonder how tall that tree is now.

We ended our trip in Tel Aviv, where I explored the White City, a unique concentration of modernist buildings created by Jewish architects who, like Mendelsohn, were fleeing

Nazi Germany. In Europe their work was scattered and they had to struggle to express themselves. Here they were given a free hand and were able realize their dreams. It shows what might have been—in Germany and other countries—had history taken a different course. I was thinking of this over dinner when Gideon's phone rang. A friend was calling to say that Yitzhak Rabin had been shot at a peace rally less than a mile away. He sat numbly, not speaking, and I shared his grief. I remembered Rabin from when he was Israeli ambassador to Washington. We even stood in line together for the Eastern Shuttle to New York, in those far off times when he didn't need a bodyguard. Now his security detail had failed him. For both of us it was the assassination of JFK once again: the death of hope, and a fatal turn for the country.

Two days later I was on the streets of the White City when sirens sounded and everyone froze for two minutes of silence. Even more moving than the broadcast of the funeral were the programs that followed. Israelis, despite their differences, are as tight-knit as a family; only the black hats failed to mourn that day. For the first time since 1963, television realized its potential to respond to a people united in sorrow. For once it was not shallow, exploitative, and voyeuristic, but healing and sincere. Leah Rabin and Shimon Peres paid their tributes. Young people sat silently holding candles, looking lost and bewildered, as an older generation sang songs of lamentation. Shalom: peace and farewell. How far has Israel fallen from the promise Rabin offered. Jewish extremists murdered British officials in the quest for independence; now their heirs occupy the seats of power, posing as great a threat to the integrity of the country as the Arabs. [1995]

Dead Sea resort

JAPAN

Mount Fuji from the Shinkansen

No country provides more surprises than Japan, and after a dozen trips I still felt as though I had strayed onto another planet. Tradition and technology are fused in an inwards-looking society that shut itself off from the outside world for three centuries and is still xenophobic. Contradictions abound: speeding on the Shinkansen through a landscape of paddy fields and smoking chimneys to sleep in a ryokan; strolling an ancient garden that's flanked with vending machines; confronting the language barrier in a country where only Japanese is spoken but English signs abound. Foreigners are treated with exquisite politeness, but the gaijin are secretly perceived as red-faced barbarians.

Himeiji Castle

In 1978, my friend Patrick Macrory took a sabbatical from his legal practice to teach law in Tokyo, and invited me to stay with his family. I flew over by Cathay Pacific; the screening of *Oh God!* was partially obscured by the shaven heads of five Buddhist monks in the front row. A day after arrival we were off, exploring the newly completed megastructures of Kenzo Tange, ancient temples, and the craft stores of Akasuka. There, I bought a hand-painted kite from an old man with a wispy white beard, and a T-shirt

Kite-maker Tasho Hakimoto; Japlish adds cachet

that read: LET'S SPORTS VIOLENT EVERY DAY. I was also taken with the jacket of a student that read "We girl are lovers of novelty and full of curiosity. The hour has struck for our departure. Since 1976."

In contrast to this Dada doggerel is the pervasive sense of order. Commuters line up behind signs on station platforms, like actors hitting their marks, waiting for the cue to enter jam-packed carriages, and then dozing on their feet. Uniforms are ubiquitous, from gray-suited salary men to tiny children in brightly colored hats. Golf driving ranges loom above the rooftops like drift nets and aficionados who could never afford a club membership practice their strokes on residential streets. Young women bow and squeak like automata in the department stores and elevators. Do they regain their humanity when they are off-duty? The basement food departments of the big stores are a treat for the senses, offering a cornucopia of produce, including musk melons that sell for $100 and are intended as gifts, not to be eaten. There's a cacophony of cries as the staff clamor for attention, extolling the qualities of whatever they are selling.

Underlying this regimentation, there's a feeling of vulnerability. Tokyo as *Metropolis*, throbbing with energy; a multi-level city of elevated railways and freeways soaring over a ganglia of wires, pipelines, and storage tanks. I could only imagine the impact of an earthquake on this fragile construction: the ruptured pipes and raging fires that would ensue, the stampede of panicked residents.

One morning we rose before dawn to visit Tskuji, the vast fish market that may soon be relocated like the wholesale markets of London and Paris. Forty years ago, visitors were toler-

Tskuji market: tuna auction, ready to go

ated as long as they stayed clear of the porters rushing around with tiers of baskets on their heads. Little Cecily—then a baby in a stroller, now an opera singer—caused a major disruption. Porters stopped to coo at this apparition; one lost his balance and shed his load of octopus in a slippery cascade. We hurried on to the quayside where tuna, bonita, and swordfish were lined up in rows, frosty skins gleaming in the first light. Buyers with flashlights peered closely, light, sniffing at the small cuts in each trunk. At 5:30, the auctioneers rang handbells and the sales began. Five minutes of performance art, the auctioneers bobbing and weaving as they yelled out the prices, the buyers gesturing frantically, as prices rose to thousands of dollars for each trophy. We adjourned to the retail market next door, marveling at fishy still-lifes and joining the porters for a breakfast of sashimi and miso soup. [1978]

On a later trip I stayed in a monastery, sleeping on a futon, serenaded to sleep by the television game shows to which novices and abbot alike were addicted. I preferred to speculate on the neighboring guests who provided shadow plays on the shoji screens. It was April, the cherry blossoms were blooming and every tree had been staked out for a group of friends or office workers. Overnight it snowed, and children in brightly colored sweaters and scarves romped in the whiteness, even as the placeholders for each tree huddled under blankets while awaiting the sake party that would follow.

I took the Shinkansen from Tokyo to explore the temples of Kyoto. Daitokuji is a complex of dry zen gardens, with mossy rocks rising from raked gravel, like forested islands in a rippling ocean. Ryogen-in, Daisen-in, Zuioho-in, and Hoshin-in: each varies in size and configuration, abstracting nature and demanding patient contemplation. A sign invites

Late snowfall in Akasuka; Cherry blossoms in Ueno Park

Shugaku-in walk garden

Raikyu-ji is a peaceful retreat

guests to participate: "Sweeping, scrubbing, wood-chopping, weed-pulling: Daisen-in will accept your labor of love if you would like a practical taste of zen."

The Moss Temple (Kokedera) demands advance reservations and asks visitors to spend 45 minutes on their knees, chanting a Buddhist mantra and tracing a sacred text with brush and ink, before they are allowed to stroll around the garden. It's an excruciating ordeal for a gaijin – will I be admitted if my calligraphy falls short? Finally, we are released to stroll around a lake surrounded by up to a hundred different mosses, mirroring red and yellow maples in its still waters. It's a Japanese miniature of Stourhead in England.

Student army on the march in Kyoto

Other gardens are secular works of art. The Imperial walk gardens of Katsura and Shugaku-in are dynamic compositions that change as you move through them on prescribed routes, with teahouses to provide points of focus like the obelisks and follies in a Western landscape garden. Visitors are marshaled through with a relentless commentary; it's more rewarding to experience one that isn't controlled by the Imperial Household Agency, such as Ritsurin Koen in Takamatsu, or Suizen-ji Koen with its miniature of Mount Fuji in Kumamoto.

There are scores of notable gardens in Kyoto alone, but the more celebrated ones are overwhelmed by school parties and tour groups, amplified commentaries, and guides' loud-hailers. For tranquility and perfection of form, I escaped to Raikyu-ji, a temple garden in the small town of Bitchu-Takahashi, two hours away by train. The temple was founded in 1339; the garden was created in the early 17th century by Enshu Kobori, a celebrated poet, calligrapher, and landscape designer. He had a hand in Daitokuji and Katsura, but this is his masterpiece. Contemporaries in England and France were carving privet bushes into pyramids and cylinders. Kobori had a freer hand, shaping a hedge to resemble a great wave or a writhing dragon. This sculptured mass leads the eye to borrowed scenery beyond, and frames a dry garden where rocks evoke tortoises and cranes, the Chinese symbols of longevity. The garden was created to delight the scholar and enlighten the seeker of wisdom, but even the uninitiated can appreciate the artistry. [2001]

SPECTACLE

There's a festival (matsuri) almost every day of the year in some part of Japan and I was lucky enough to catch one of the best on my first visit. Every May 18th in Nikko, an hour -long train ride north of Tokyo, a thousand locals re-enact the procession that brought the remains of Tokugawa Ieyasu to his mausoleum four centuries ago. Ieysu founded the Shogunate and wanted to be remembered as a divinity. His son built the opulent shrine and was later interred there himself. Nothing could be further removed from zen restraint than this polychrome and gold bestiary of monkeys and birds, lions and dragons, set on stone terraces amid the cryptomerias.

Lunch break

Mounted archers launch the ceremony the previous day, and the parade features samurai in full armor, children in golden headdresses, priests, fairies, falconers, a sacred tree, and a full supporting cast in gorgeous colors. During the lunch break, the spell is broken as the participants light up and munch on rice cakes, samurai allow their girlfriends to try on their helmets, and children tote their Mickey Mouse thermoses. A marshal gives the command to saddle-up, and the army retraces its steps. I looked for the director to call "action" in this scene from a period epic.

On a later trip I took a local train from Kyoto to the mountain village of Kurama, for the October 22nd fire festival. As darkness falls, flaming torches are carried along the main street to the shrine to propitiate the gods. Local trains bring crowds of outsiders but it's a ceremony deeply rooted in this community of 600. The preparations are as elaborate as the event itself. Giant torches of willow, loosely bound with twigs, are stacked in an open space at the foot of the hill. Zig-zag folds of white paper are suspended from bare branches to attract friendly spirits (kami). Homeowners open doors and shutters to display

Tosho-gu festival: parade

Preparing for Tosho-gu; Kurama-Hi fire festival

ornate shrines, paper lanterns, a brasier for warmth, and a bucket of water to extinguish embers. Firemen crouch watchfully in side alleys, hoses ready.

Robert Singer, Curator of Japanese Art at the LA County Museum of Art, introduced me to Yohko Hayashi, a graphic designer whose family has lived on the main street for generations. He laid out a buffet for twenty friends: freshwater shrimp, soup of langoustes, pickled fish and rice, stir-fried vegetables, beef in mustard sauce, and plenty to drink. As darkness fell, young men stripped to a loin cloth and a skirt of cords. Well-fortified with sake, they lighted their torches at the brasiers and trotted off down the hill in a cloud of sparks. Our host changed from his red-checkered shirt and baggy pants to samurai robes and disappeared for much of the evening. Fire and feasting alternated through the evening, as we emerged to cheer the runners on their way. By now children had joined in and the entire village was *en fête*, the street glowing from the flames and dense with smoke. As midnight approached, the fires ebbed, and we joined the line for the last train back to Kyoto.

The Japanese love to dress up, and seize every opportunity to do so. On Sundays, working-class kids who spend their weekdays in menial jobs, rally at Hanraku Park, stuff everyday clothes into bags, and reappear as mods and rockers or in punk gear to dance around a boom box. It's a protest against conformity in which the participants dress and dance exactly alike. The first time I caught this celebration, parents were bringing their small children to the Meiji Shrine for 3-5-7 day, an annual treat for boys of three and seven and girls of five. Traditional robes alternated with Victorian attire and each child clutched a tote bag of thousand-year candy and good-luck charms. The contrast between these pampered darlings and the brazen teenagers was surreal.

Dressing up in Tokyo: rockers at Hanraku Park

No festival can match the spectacle and skill of kabuki, and the place to see it is the Kabuki-za theater in Tokyo, sitting high up in the gallery amid the claques who have come to cheer their favorite actor. Kabuki began as a people's theater, a subversive mix of comedy and melodrama that offered a welcome alternative to the solemnity of Noh. As in Shakespeare's day, all roles are played by men, and they have stage names that are carried forward from one generation to the next. Fans shout these names to encourage or applaud their favorites. A play runs five hours with two long intervals for the sale of bentos, and an earphone translation brings the complex plots alive. Tearful partings alternate with slapstick and acrobatic fights. A hero leaps onto a roof to evade his foes, ghosts and skeletons drag a villain down to hell, snow flutters from above, and a clock is lowered to indicate the time. Dazzling costumes are changed at lightning speed, stylized sets extend the full width of the stage, and the lighting effects are spectacular. Kabuki exploits the full resources of live theater. [1980/2007]

7-5-3 day

PUPPETS ON KYUSHU

What drew me back to Japan every couple of years was the juxtaposition of the very old and very new. In the rural heart of Kyushu, the south island, there's a complex of new wooden buildings that sustain the local tradition of Bunraku puppet theater. I went to Seiwa Bunka with the Tokyo-based architect, Kazuhiro Ishii, for a leisurely lunch, a walk around the museum, shopping for local crafts, and a performance in the intimate auditorium. The throng of Japanese tourists seems to take everything for granted, but I'm in heaven. As the only Westerner there, I've found something I'm always searching for: a perfect balance of the innovative and the timeless. Ishii is inspired by ancient barns and temples but he uses computer software to assemble beams of aromatic cedar, fitting them together without nails in complex geometrical patterns. A self-supporting frame of stripped pine logs is covered with a translucent membrane to house the octagonal restaurant. The other buildings have cat's-cradle roof vaults that support heavy gray tiles.

I cleaned out my bento, a two-tier lacquered box containing succulent morsels of river fish and mountain greens, yams, rice, and puckery plums. We walked around the display

Seiwa Bunka Bunraku puppet theater

of articulated wooden heads, hands, and legs, plus the elaborate costumes that conceal the tapes linking these extremities. Now it's time to take our seats and watch the show. The stage is broad and horizontal as in Kabuki, for these two popular forms of entertainment both evolved three centuries ago. A trio of black-shrouded handlers, wearing gauze hoods to make them seem invisible, manipulate each puppet's parts with hidden levers.

Today they are staging a classic tear-jerker, *The Pilgrim's Song*, which was first performed in 1768. A woman on the run recognizes the girl singing at her gate as the daughter she was forced to abandon years before, and the girl has a feeling she has found her long-lost mother. But the pursuers are closing in, and the older woman pretends the girl is a stranger and sends her away. A young man narrates the dialogue in appropriate tones, precisely capturing the daughter's fearful simper. Half the audience is sobbing, as though these were live actors. The performance ends with a brilliant display of stagecraft, as brightly painted sets are flipped in rapid succession.

Then the hoods come off and a row of farm workers with wizened faces take a bow. Almost every day through the year, these men and women leave fields and workshops for a few hours to rehearse, perform, and instruct their children, in a tradition reaching back through the centuries. It takes many years to master the art, and they have to practice constantly to ensure that every pair of hands works in harmony. As they rehearse, their faces are a study in concentration, as impassive as the puppets are expressive. I'm reminded of Walker Evans's portraits of Dust Bowl farmers, and I ask if they feel the emotions of the characters they bring to life. They say they do, but it doesn't show.

Later, we check into An An An, a village inn located up a steep hillside trail. It was formerly a farmhouse, nearly as old as the play we just saw. The owner's wife died and now this cheerful man does everything himself, laying out the futons on tatami mats, stoking the fire under the communal tub in the courtyard, preparing a hearty dinner of local produce and grilled chicken; even playing a CD of Strauss waltzes in honor of the visiting gaijin. The former mayor, who commissioned the theater, drives over to say hello. He tells us that the center has improved the economy of Seiwa, a village of 3,000 people, and has slowed its decline. Young people feel a sense of pride in having a place outsiders travel to see, and some have put off their move to the city.

Messages to attract spirits

In the long run it's a losing battle, for all of Japan is ageing as the birth rate lags, and rural areas are the most vulnerable. That strengthens one's appreciation for a culture that's being marginalized. The authorities are vigilant in preserving a few historic villages and landmark buildings, but they've actively encouraged the wholesale destruction of wooden houses in Kyoto. In that legendary city, temples and gardens of extraordinary beauty surround a commercial center of mind-numbing ugliness. Occasionally, the two worlds interact. I once strayed into a temple garden to find it full of lights, actors in medieval

Kyoto: Nanzen-ji

Naoshima: George Rickey

costume, and the usual flock of gofers, as the director set up a scene for a period movie. In general, old buildings are fenced off as exotic survivors, to be gawked at like animals in a zoo, but rarely put to use. That makes it all the more valuable when historic villages and neighborhoods, as well as individual structures, can be given a vibrant new life and set off by the 21st century's best work.

ART ON NAOSHIMA

Over the past decade, the Benesse publishing corporation has created an art park to preserve and animate Naoshima, a small hilly island in Japan's Inland Sea. The late Tetsuhiko Fukutake was looking for a quiet place to retire and display the art he had collected as the company's CEO. To see what he and his foundation have accomplished, I took the hour-long ferry trip from the port city of Takamatsu. It was a clear, windy morning in early November, and I clung to the rail as the boat pitched and rolled. The peaks of former mountains rose from the choppy waters, layered one against another as in an ink-wash drawing. The towers of the city fell astern, tankers and freighters dissolved in the glare of the low sun, and I basked in the natural beauty of the seascape.

That made the shock of arrival all the greater. To shelter passengers, the architectural partnership of Sanaa has created a steel and glass pavilion that seems to be hovering, weightless on the quay. Large mirrors pull in the landscape and dissolve the structure. Provocative sculptures, including Yayoi Kusama's huge scarlet pumpkin, are scattered around, and abandoned houses in the village have been transformed into site-specific art works. A cobbled lane leads past wood siding that has been scorched charcoal black to reduce the risk of fire, and fenced yards ablaze with orange persimmons. In one 200-year-old house, neon numbers appear to float in a pool of water that fills most of the ground floor. Villagers were invited to choose their favorite numbers and set the speed at which they would flash. A stained

Sanaa installation

wood shed encloses a James Turrell light piece, which you dimly perceive after sitting for five minutes in total darkness. Fukutake and the Benesse Foundation that maintains his legacy commissioned the Osaka-based architect Tadao Ando to design an art museum and a luxurious guesthouse and, more recently, a waterfront hotel and a second, underground museum. A shuttle links these four buildings to the ferry, so I was spared the steep uphill climb from the hotel. Ando employs poured concrete as though it were the finest limestone to create serene galleries and architectural promenades, leading a visitor through shadowy passages to rock-filled courtyards, down darkened ramps and out to panoramic views over the island.

What makes the complex so special is the integration of art, architecture, and landscape. Kinetic steel sculptures by George Rickey waved like semaphore flags in the wind, playing off the pines silhouetted against a silvery expanse of water. In the Benesse House museum, Hiroshi Sugimoto photos of ocean horizons are displayed in a paved courtyard, preserved from fading by UV-blocking acrylic, and Richard Long's circles of stones and driftwood bring the outside in. There's an eclectic mix of leading American and Japanese artists, generously spaced.

A self-operated funicular railway carries a few lucky guests up to an oval courtyard that is enclosed by eight spacious suites. The Park Hotel offers spare rooms and an expansive restaurant looking out to sea. Ando's artistry in the Chichu museum is concealed within a grassy mound that, as you approach, reveals only skylight openings and the portal. I removed my shoes to enter a luminous white gallery, lit from above and paved with unmortared white marble tesserae. Each wall displays a large Monet canvas of water lilies so that here, as in the Orangerie in Paris, you are immersed in the world of this painter. Walter de Maria created a site-specific work that includes a polished granite sphere placed midway up a staircase ascending through a three-level hall, and you could imagine the room serving as a shrine for an eccentric cult. [2007]

CHINA

Beijing was a different city 30 years ago. The airport resembled a provincial bus station, far removed from the urban boundaries; the streets were full of buses and bikes with very few cars. Foreigners were segregated in special waiting areas and the gloomy upstairs rooms of restaurants. Visiting the Temple of Heaven, I found myself surrounded by a circle of peasants, up for day of sightseeing in the capital, staring at me with intense curiosity as though I were a Martian. The alleys (hutongs) were still overflowing with life, a barber trimmed children's hair on a street corner, and a hot-potato seller did a brisk trade. At a neighborhood market, old men carried songbirds on twigs and their arias competed with the twittering of crickets in pierced gourds. Tianan'men on a Sunday afternoon was full of families flying kites, as cheerful and spontaneous as the Zocalo in Mexico City, with no premonition of the mass demonstrations and massacre of the following year.

One night, after dinner at one of the few foreign-owned hotels, I wandered off on deserted streets in search of the traditional Peking Opera. I entered a cavernous hall and paid the equivalent of a nickel to join old men sitting on benches and cheering the performers. It was a proletarian crowd in Mao jackets and caps, and they were probably here a decade earlier watching Jiang Qing's *The Red Detachment of Women*, or another of her agit-prop ballets. I'm sure this decadent fare was much more to their taste: gorgeously robed lords and retainers, bearded clowns, a girl disguised as a pink and green scallop doing high kicks. Thrilling acrobatics were accompanied by singing that had the shrill dissonances of a cat fight. Like the puppet theater in Palermo, it was still in full flow an hour or two later as I retreated into the night.

From Beijing I traveled on to Shanghai and took a day trip to Suzhou, an hour away by train. The city was founded in 500 BC, flourished for centuries as a center of trade and scholarship, and was praised by Marco Polo in 1276 as "a noble city and great" with 6,000 stone bridges – or so he said. There are now a million people living in a drab sprawl of post-revolutionary buildings, but a few of the canals survive, and it preserves a dozen walled gardens that resemble three-dimensional Chinese scrolls. Several were designed by landscape painters who recreated mountains, forests, and lakes on a miniature scale, borrowing real landscapes from over the walls. They served as retreats for scholars and cultured officials who would invite friends over to compose poems or admire particularly elaborate rocks, while drinking wine and listening to the sounds of lute and flute. Today, these oases can be mobbed in high season, but on this first trip I found only a few old men, gossiping and soaking up the pale sun.

Beijing: Summer Palace, itinerant barber in a hutong

Timeless serenity of Suzhou's gardens in winter

Moon gates frame pools and pavilions in a Suzhou garden

Traditional gardens are tightly compressed and meant to be experienced one vista at a time. The walls symbolize infinity like the blank areas of a scroll. Together with the still pools, they serve as a foil to walkways that rise and fall, twist and turn. Grilles and moon gates compel you to pause and contemplate what lies beyond. Pebbles and cobbles are arranged to form patterned pavements. The strongest elements are the rocks, which were submerged in running water to create expressive hollows, then wrapped in silk for transport. Each garden employs similar elements to create a different effect. Together they recall a long-vanished era of learning, pleasure, and delight.

On a later visit I escaped the crowds in the new art museum created by I.M. Pei who was born in Suzhou to a family that was here a thousand years before. The architect was tempted out of retirement to design a building of black and white stone that abstracts the local vernacular. Like the gardens, it offers constantly shifting perspectives and an architectural promenade. [1988]

***

Today's China is all about the new. The Red Guards of the Cultural Revolution were urged to smash the old; what little survived from the past is overwhelmed by tour groups. Historical buildings have been rebuilt or over-restored. Happily, talented architects from around the world are creating a new architectural legacy. Norman Foster's Beijing Airport Terminal is a mile across and brilliantly organized. The Shanghai district of Pudong resembles a futuristic movie set, especially at night. The high rises of Shenzen and Guangzhou make Manhattan skyscrapers look old-fashioned.

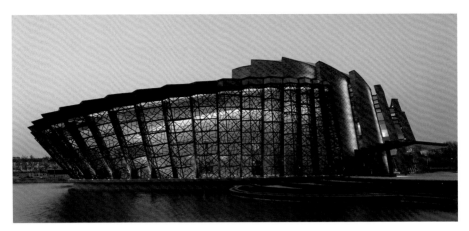

Wuzhen: theater and (below) canal houses

Even more remarkable is the rise of young Chinese architects. Wang Shu and Lou Wen, a husband and wife who practice together as Amateur Architecture, showed me over the new Xiangshan campus of the China Art Academy, outside Hangzhou. Wang was only 39 when he won this prestigious commission; 10 years later he won the Pritzker Prize. Until the 1990s, everything was done by one of the huge state institutes—lumbering dinosaurs that still get most of the big jobs—along with starchitects from the West. As Wang told me, "the old guard still wields power, but a new generation and new styles of expression are emerging." The campus is a fusion of old and new; gray, clay bricks and tiles from demolished buildings artfully reassembled in structures that reinterpret traditional forms. They respond to the landscape and are as harmonious in their configuration as the calligraphy that Wang loves to practice.

A two hour drive away is Wuzhen, a canal town that was half destroyed by fire in 1999 and reconstructed at the expense of Xiang Hong Chen, a local boy who made a fortune. From a boat on a rainy night it becomes a work of art. The buildings are varied, beautifully detailed, and skillfully lit. Bridges vary from high arches to simple slabs of stone, willows emerge from the mist. In the early morning, before the tour buses arrived, I admired the finely crafted gray clay roof tiles, fretted screens, and low carved stone reliefs.

That traditional vocabulary inspired the theater that Chen commissioned from Kris Yao, the leading architect of Taiwan. Canted and curved walls have gray stone edges and boarded sides; the entry foyer is lit from expansive glazing with a "broken ice" screen of reclaimed wood. A broad concourse of figured white marble surrounds the main theater, seating 1,100, and the black box seating 200, which are linked by their stages. The walls of the main theater are clad in a repoussé fabric, the small theater with gold mesh. Regretably, this treasure is rarely used outside of the September theater festival. [2015]

SAMARKAND AND BUKHARA

Samarkand: Bread vendors in bazaar

I had long dreamed of visiting Bukhara and Samarkand, legendary stops on the Silk Road, and my chance came when I flew to Tashkent from Istanbul. It was a revealing trip: newly independent Uzbekistan replaying the Soviet tragedy as farce; Marx ceding place to the Marx Brothers. Flights from the West to Tashkent arrive at 2:30 am. The passport examination was grimly familiar from Cold War days, only now it's not a search for spies, but a struggle to read the passport entries. After five minutes of turning the pages, the callow recruit raised his stamp. It froze in mid-air. Had something incriminating been found? No, it was just for effect. Down it thumped, and I was over the first hurdle. Then came the currency check. Count every coin and fill in the amounts in triplicate, in figures and letters in microscopic spaces. Any mistake and one is sent back to do it again. I was reminded of the kanji-copying exercise at the Moss Temple. Finally, my calculations were approved and the forms were filed away, never to be seen again.

And now a final challenge. Would Bahodir, the local rep of the Aga Khan Trust be there to meet me, as promised. A predatory horde of drivers pressed forward. No sign of my host. I affected indifference. Half an hour passed, the remaining passengers emerged and were carried off into the night. Finally Bahodir drove up in his late-model Renault (business must be good; with taxes and bribes this had to have cost him at least $80,000) and we took a scenic tour of Taskent: one masterpiece of socialist architecture after another. How could I muster enthusiasm? Luckily they were all dim shadows so I felt no need to pretend. We reached the bus station, where the drivers were all asleep and had lower expectations than those at the airport. Bahodir promised $40 for Samarkand – an eight-hour round-trip. The driver was too dazed to object (he shouldn't; in greenbacks it's more than he'll make all week from local fares).

Off we set at breathtaking speed, undeterred by the dense fog, alternately on high beam, (which blinds the driver) and no beam; there seemed to be nothing in between.

Samarkand: Gur Emir

Bukhara: Ismail Samani Mausoleum

The newly reconstructed Ark of Bukhara

Happily there was little traffic and the center line showed faintly through the murk. After two hours of hunkering down in the back seat, resisting invitations to sit up front while thinking of Princess Di's sad fate, the fog began to lift at dawn. Now our progress was slowed by police speed traps—two cigarettes is the standard pay-off—and the opportunities to buy little bottles of gasoline and a sack of apples from roadside merchants. Finally we arrived at Samarkand's Afrosyob Hotel, a monstrous caravanserai built by the Soviets (with a striving for effect and no thought of comfort) for the expected flood of Russian tourists. Now they can head West, the appeal of this outpost has shrunk. Few rooms were occupied and the marble halls were deserted.

The richly tiled mosque and madrassas of the Registan have been over-restored, giving them the unreality of a movie set. Communism has yielded to nationalism, and statues of Lenin have been replaced by those of Tamerlane, who achieved an even larger body count during his bloody reign, but is now venerated as a patriot. I went to see his resting place and insisted on seeing the real thing, concealed in a basement beneath the marble catafalque. I had to wait until a group of officials moved out and, in my eagerness get in before the chamber closed, I tripped and fell, nearly joining Tamerlane in his tomb.

The Aga Khan's architect in Samarkand was Tony, a Marxist stone mason from Yorkshire who helped restore Wells Cathedral and Westminster Abbey. He was patiently retrofitting an old courtyard house to demonstrate adaptive reuse to the locals, even as they practiced their own version of urban renewal by bulldozing a whole row of houses across the street. That has been going on for a long time to judge from the acres of open space in the city center. Undeterred, Tony went off to help patch up a mosque in a neighborhood that seemed to be vanishing like a sand castle at high tide.

Another cut-price jalopy took me to Bukhara, where the old walled city has preserved its mud-brick courtyard houses and labyrinth of dusty lanes. Old men lounged on bed-like couches in a shady square, playing dominoes in the shade of gnarled mulberry trees. The Ismail Samani Mausoleum is a masterpiece of patterned brick from the 12th century, concealed in the ground for centuries, before it was excavated and improved in 1934. Urban renewal is confined to the reconstruction of the citadel, which is now gleamingly new. I walked into the principal mosque and found myself in the middle of a rehearsal for

Rehearsing the 2,500-year anniversary celebration of Bukhara

a pageant, celebrating the city's 2,500-year anniversary. Such a nice round number, just as the regime needs a distraction from quotidian problems, and how convenient that it's the 2,500th birthday of Khiva, too, just a year after Tamerlane's anniversary in Samarkand.

Let's put on a show to impress our foreign guests, and draw a veil over the centuries of rape, pillage, and destruction. How about young women in chiffon tunics fluttering their arms in the air and waving fans? Toreadors with red capes, and gypsies straight out of *Carmen* (just the thing for Japanese tour groups) and army recruits with pennants waving from pointy hats. Throw in a handful of emirs with long white beards, and an MC with a sonorous voice – the kind who narrates trailers for art films. The director—raging, stomping, and tearing his hair at every miscue—was more fun to watch than the cast, but the spectacle probably looked better when floodlit at night. A French journalist advised me that this event was limited to foreigners and high officials; locals were instructed to stock up and stay home for the weekend.

Wandering back to my hotel, I found myself in a cul-de-sac. Three toughs pointed at my camera, inviting me to come closer, and I saw no escape. Other Englishmen came to a miserable end in Bukhara and I feared I would be added to the roster. Should I hand over the camera, full of precious shots, and run? At that moment, a dozen army recruits on a field exercise scrambled over a wall and marched past. I fell into step behind them and withdrew with my military escort. [1999]

MEXICO

Staying at the Majestic Hotel in Mexico City gives you a front row view of the Zocalo, the largest plaza in the Americas, and a stage for great events and everyday life. Every morning at 6 am troops march out from the National Palace, form a square, and raise a huge flag.

A cast-iron bandstand is the centerpiece of the zocalo in Oaxaca

In Vera Cruz, children appropriate the stage

A band blares, swords flash, and troops salute then march away. Rockets explode from the roof of the palace. Or so it happened when I was first there. Aztec priests and Spanish conquistadores performed equally solemn rituals on or near this site, the symbolic heart of a city that was founded six centuries ago.

Back then, mariachi musicians waited for clients in the Plaza Garibaldi. A dozen letter writers plied their trade in the arcades of the Plaza de Santo Domingo, composing romantic epistles, job applications, and pleas to officials, and banging them out on beat-up Remingtons. Surely they've been superseded by texts on smart phones. I was lucky to catch the end of an era, when the plaza, large or small, was the social and political hub of every community. Created by the Spanish as symbols of authority, they embody Mexicans' love of conviviality and spectacle. Some, like the Zócalo have been paved; others, inspired by 19th-century Paris, have become parks.

To research a book, *The City Square*, I drove around the country, from the capital, south to Oaxaca and Guadalajara. I spent a whole day in the Plaza de la Borda of Taxco, a level space in the steep labyrinth of a city that grew rich on silver. Restaurants, bars and shops flank the towering Churrigueresque church of Santa Prisca. At 8 am on a cool winter morning, a small boy is sweeping the leaves with a birch broom, and another is dragging a reluctant pig to market. A dozen stray dogs patrol the square and children hurry to school.

As the tempo increases so does the noise. Fireworks explode to inaugurate a fiesta; later come church bells, more fireworks, and an off-key band. An elderly cop lets off piercing blasts on his whistle, not to direct traffic but to advertise his role as a parking attendant. Drivers pull over to chat, further tangling the traffic. At 1 pm, children return from school and fill the plaza before hurrying home for lunch. As the hours pass, old men take the sun, families gather, and finally it becomes a rendezvous for teenagers.

All that's lacking is the Sunday evening paseo, which I experienced in San Miguel de Allende. By 8 pm every bench in the Jardin de Allende was full and the mating dance began. Girls paraded counter-clockwise around the plaza, arm in arm and three abreast, gossiping but watchful, in a progress as brisk as a cotillion. Boys made a perfunctory clockwise movement, but most darted into line to walk with the girls or draw them aside. Foreigners and couples threaded in between, balloon sellers worked the families on the benches, a band blasted away from the kiosk. Nothing slowed the youthful carousel, which revolved late into the night. [1988]

* * *

Luis Barragán built very little during his last 40 years in Mexico City, but each project is a portrait of an inspired architect who had the means and will to follow his solitary path. The elemental simplicity of his houses is a fusion of modernism and the rural vernacular, mass and void, rough plaster and refined proportions. On a recent trip, I was able to visit four of them by appointment. The architect moved from his home city of Guadalajara in the early 1940s and spent the rest of his life in the Casa Barragán. Behind its anonymous exterior little has changed since his death in 1985, thanks to the housekeeper, Ana Luisa.

A lofty living room doubles as an office, littered with books and papers, and a cross of glazing bars divides a wall of glass that frames the jungle-like garden. Stairs of black volcanic rock are lit from above, and the eye is drawn up to a gold canvas by Mathias Goeritz, a close associate of Barragán. A simple wood side-chair from a farmhouse kitchen is set off by a bright pink wall. The bedroom is spartan and a crucifix hangs over the single bed. Barragan was a devout catholic and I remember a whip and scourge from an earlier visit, but this has been edited out. In the studio, cantilevered wood treads lead up to a roof terrace that is fully enclosed by colored walls.

The other houses play variations on these themes. Casa Prieto is the largest and was meant to be a model for Jardines de Pedregal, a planned community that would respond to the volcanic rockscape south of the city. In contrast to the others, the colors are subdued: dusty pink, gray, and blue. Jorge Covarrubias, the architect who restored the house for a new owner, insists that "Barragan is not about color but atmosphere. Choices had to be made – not always the first layer of paint." Living spaces flow into each other as the house steps

Luis Barragan's indoor pool for the Gilardi House

Fountain for Los Clubes

down a slope from the entry court to a pool court with rock outcrops. Light reflected off walls inflects their color, turning pink to pale blue-gray. The shifts of level and generous proportions, broad pine floor boards and massive wood furniture give this house the elemental quality that characterizes Barragan's best work.

The Cuadra San Cristobal is located in a northern suburb of Mexico City. On the tedious drive out you pass the cluster of colored obelisks that Goeritz designed for Satellite City, another planned development that was hijacked by speculators. The Egerstroms, a Swedish couple who loved horses, commissioned a modest white house and an expansive stable yard in the gated community of Los Clubes. Pink walls are cut away to frame the house and are highlighted by panels of blue and violet, with a row of stables to one side. A cantilevered conduit gushes water into a shallow pool: an image that has long defined Barragán to the world. Just up the street is a similar spout and pool to serve horsey neighbors.

Barragán came out of retirement to design a double town house for the Gilardi family, and the present owner, Martin Luque, allows visitors to immerse themselves in fields of vibrant color as they explore the ground-floor rooms. A gallery with yellow-lined openings opens onto an indoor pool with blue walls and an intense red shaft. A ray of sunlight creates a diagonal accent. The richly grained stone floors resemble wood. A glass door opens onto the central patio, which was built around a jacaranda tree, with a blue wall that merges into the sky, and another of pink. Unrailed, polished wood stairs lead up to a living room that opens onto a little courtyard and a library. At every turn, shutters open to reveal another vista. [2017]

Atlantida: Edificio Planeto a streamline apartment block

MODERNIST URUGUAY

The late Fernando Vasquez, a good friend and talented architect, wanted me to see the rich legacy of modernism in his native city of Montevideo, and arranged for me to fly down there. I stayed with his mother, conversing in a jumble of languages since she had never mastered English and I seem unable to learn Spanish. Architects showed me around the city, extolling their favorites, and my visit was well timed. The mayor, Mariano Arana, an architect and urbanist, was eager to save the buildings constructed in the prosperous decades of the 1930s and 1940s, which were now at risk from redevelopment, as Uruguay recovered from a half century of economic decline.

For a week, I wandered around in a happy daze, finding treasures on every block. Uruguay celebrated its centennial of independence in 1930 and decided to embrace modernism as a badge of progress. That marked it off from Argentina, its deeply conservative neighbor, and provided an opportunity for two generations of creative architects. Remoteness from centers of innovation allowed these local talents to develop strange variations on the fashionable International and streamline modern styles. Buildings for government and industry are rigorously geometrical, the police kiosks along the waterfront take their cues from the waves, and apartment buildings indulge every kind of fantasy.

War halted new construction in Europe and the US; here it continued to flourish, and mutate. Shabby as many streets have become, they offer a time capsule comparable to that of Miami's South Beach, or Asmara in Eritrea. Here, the diversity is much greater, and one can trace the echoes of De Stijl, Le Corbusier, and the rich ornamentation of Parisian Art

Eladio Dieste's Workers' Church in Atlantida

Déco. Elliptical balconies are enriched with angular, curvilinear and floral balustrades, rooftop pergolas, and expressive entrance canopies.

One name stands out in the post-war era: the engineer-turned-architect Eladio Dieste. His masterpiece is the Workers' Church at Atlantida, midway between Montevideo and the smart resort of Punta del Este. Dieste's signature material was brick and he used it with the same sculptural flair as Félix Candela employed concrete in Mexico, for sculptural walls and roof vaults. The side walls of the church undulate and flare, seeming to stretch the entry facade to a taut screen. Another church progressed no further than a huge curved apse, but some of the same exuberance is found in his warehouses, a shopping mall and other secular structures.

I was granted a brief meeting with Dieste, a frail octogenarian sitting at home in pajamas and barely whispering his responses. The architect's companion asked me not to tire him, but he seemed to welcome the opportunity to talk about his work with an enthusiast. His eyes twinkled and he covered the page of a notebook with figures, as though calculating the stresses on a future building. He made everything sound easy, the product of intuition rather than calculation, but it's easy to see how challenging it must have been to build this way before the advent of computer software. [1998]

CUBA

At the end of 2000, I joined a small group on a two-week trip to Cuba, flying via Cancun and claiming an affiliation with the Sephardic Friendship Society. These Jewish philanthropists were exempt from the travel ban on US citizens, and—though we never met up—they provided us with cover for our architectural odyssey, and my companions' shared passion for watercolors.

I knew I would find a country caught in a time warp, a decaying paradise of crumbling mansions occupied by a dozen families and Detroit dreamboats defying their age, but the physical reality was far more intense than I expected. We celebrated New Year at a wild party in the main square (remembering what happened that night in 1958–59), and vibrated to the beat of santeria dances at a nightclub called Las Vegas. We climbed the tottering stairs of La Guardarita, one of several *paladeres*—private houses that are allowed to serve meals to a dozen guests—and ate extraordinarily well. Reservations are coveted, for most government-owned restaurants offer tough chicken, Bulgarian wine, and indifferent service.

Ordinary Cubans stand in long lines to buy the basics with an almost valueless currency, and get around town in camels—pink cattle trucks, packed to bursting point. Strident slogans—"Patria o Muerte" and "Viva la Revolucion Socialista" mock the material failings of Castro's state, and distract from the polarization of wealth between Westerners and Cubans that has become almost as extreme as it was in the Batista era. El Jefe would grind his teeth in rage if he knew how enthusiastically the Yanquis are greeted.

The colonial core of Havana, tarted up with acrylic paint to please the tourists, offered few surprises, but the concentration of modernism from the 1940s and 1950s was astonishing. As in Montevideo, progressive styles were eagerly embraced in those decades – for apartment towers, public buildings, and middle-class villas (whose owners fled to Miami). Few other cities have come close to this passion for the spirit of the age. We scrambled through puddles and cobwebs in the Art Schools, a post-revolutionary project that seemed as abandoned as a lost city in the jungle. Eduardo Luis Rodriguez (who authored the definitive *Havana Guide*) took us through the sensuously curved Club Nautico, La Moderna Poesia (a tower as poetic as its name), and the America movie palace, a sleeping beauty I longed to awake with a program of Hollywood musicals. I could imagine the ecstatic response to Fred Astaire partnering Rita Hayworth in Cole Porter's *So Near and Yet So Far*.

Public transportation in Havana; Roadside exhortation

Havana modern: Collegio d'Arquitectura

Havana: Eugenio Leal House

The highlight of our trip was Trinidad, a UNESCO World Heritage site. The town grew rich from the yield of sugar mills through the 19th century but then went into a long slumber. Anywhere else in the Americas such a gem would be a parking lot for cars and tour buses, and the main street would be lined with souvenir shops and plastic signs. Nothing disturbed the tranquility of Trinidad at sunset but a couple of cowboys from the sugar plantations clip-clopping over the cobbles, and some musicians warming up for an evening gig. Faces appeared behind the window grilles but the streets remained empty. Next day, the town came alive, and the architect who showed us the buildings he had restored stopped a hundred times to hug his neighbors. Here in the country, we could recapture the lazy, pre-revolutionary rhythms of Cuba, where people may make a living from the land and ignore the sloganeering. [2000–01]

Trinidad: cobbled streets and window grilles

Oscar Niemeyer's art museum at Niteroi

BRAZIL

I first went to Brazil in 1971 when filmmakers and musicians were finding inventive ways to tweak the noses of the military junta and avoid censorship. Monday through Friday I selected movies—*How Tasty was my Little Frenchman* was a great find—for a program in Washington, and nights I went to concerts by Antônio Carlos Jobim, Maria Bethânia, Baden Powell, and other greats, where young audiences sang the lyrics of banned songs as the musicians played along. At weekends I joined a couple of journalists at noon, spending a few hours on a specific stretch of Leblon Beach in company with their professional peers. Back for lunch at 4, a long siesta in their cool apartment and then to dinner around 11. Four years later I returned and knew I would find them at the same spot, chatting away to friends and ignoring the nubile bodies playing paddle ball. I made an excursion to the newly completed center of Brasilia and drove south from Rio to meet Roberto Burle Marx, the white haired maestro of landscape design.

Those brief encounters inspired a later trip to explore the work of Oscar Niemeyer, the architect who embodied the sensual Carioca spirit and put Brazil on the international map.

In 1939, when he was completing designs for the Ministry of Education and Health in downtown Rio, I could have flown there from New York on the Pan American Clipper, landing in the bay beside the Sugar Loaf mountain. Today, the flight is prosaic, though much faster, and you reach the waterfront though a decayed and horrendously congested city. Happily, the essentials haven't changed. My taxi raced along the waterfront, skirting the promenade with its undulating mosaic waves, and the terminal where the flying boats used to dock.

Health has been supplanted by Culture, and the Ministry has been renamed Palacio Gustavo Capanema for the progressive politician who threw out the retro competition-winning design of 1935, and hired a bunch of adventurous young architects.

Parliament in Brasilia

They turned for help to their hero, Le Corbusier, and the great Swiss form-giver sketched a design that Niemeyer fleshed out. It's a classic statement of modernist principles: a curtain-walled slab of offices raised on pilotis over a low wing that extends back to define a plaza.

Louvers shade the facade and blue and white ceramic seahorses and ships pattern the solid walls. Only the lobby and mezzanine gallery are open to the public but I was lucky enough to find the young woman who is responsible for the maintenance of the building. "Everyone else is on strike today," she explained, "But I have a responsibility to be here." She showed me through the richly paneled offices of the minister—a position now held by Carlos Jobim—and the reception areas where the art, furnishings, and carpets seem caught

Rio: Leblon beach

in a time warp, and on to the roof terrace from where I could look down on the swirling paths and plantings of Burle Marx's gardens.

In the early 1940s, Juscelino Kubitschek, the mayor of Belo Horizonte, commissioned Niemeyer to upgrade this provincial capital, by creating four buildings to spur a new development around Pampulha Lake. The casino (now a museum of modern art), dance hall, yacht club, and church were sketched in a night and they gave birth to a new language of Brazilian architecture, a tropical modernism in which every line swells and flows. After seeing the designs, Le Corbusier declared: "Oscar, you have Rio's mountains in your eyes!" Ten years later, Niemeyer designed a house for himself in the densely wooded mountains behind Rio. The Casa de Canoas is maintained by the architect's foundation and nothing seems to have changed since he lived here. Three flat, rounded planes project out like the leaves of a shamrock to shade terraces and curved glass windows that frame views of mountains, forest, and distant ocean.

Brasilia overshadows Niemeyer's other work, but I was intrigued by a trio of innovative structures in Sao Paulo, an intimidatingly huge metropolis that—like Mexico City—is redeemed by its energy and rich cultural life. The sinuous lines of Copan, a huge apartment building, and the inter-twined ramps that link the different levels of the Oca and Biennale pavilions, were enough to justify the trip. Back in Rio I took a ferry across the bay to the Niteroi art museum. Its terrace commands a panoramic view and a ramp coils up to the entry of this spectacular white mushroom. [2006]

Niemeyer's apartment tower in Belo Horizonte

TRANSFORMING MEDELLIN

Three decades ago, Colombia was as crime-ridden as Venezuela is today, and Medellin, the second largest city, was torn apart by drug violence. By 2010, Pablo Escobar was dead, and the gangs subdued. That year I went to explore new architecture and discovered a city trans-formed. Architects of different generations were eager to collaborate on public projects and even work pro bono. Progressive mayors had enlisted their support and empowered them to enhance the livability and self-esteem of the poorest barrios.

The Orquideorama in the Botanical Garden of Medellin

Medellin: cable car

As recently as 2003, the hillside slum of Santo Domingo was a no-go zone for outsiders, and even residents were advised to stay off streets controlled by urban militias. A systematic program of urban improvements changed all that. An elevated Metrorail bisects the city, north to south, and cable cars skim over the steep slopes at either end.

The nighttime ascent to Santo Domingo is as breathtaking as the opening scene of *Blade Runner*. The city below becomes a glittering carpet of lights, the descending cars whirl silently by, and the three black crystals of Giancarlo Mazzanti's Biblioteca de España glow enticingly from the edge of an escarpment. Stations are extraordinarily clean and well-maintained and young attendants help passengers to board. Strangers greet each other as they take their seats, eight to a car. As we climbed, I could hear the sounds of children playing and dogs barking, and glimpse a candlelit procession wending its way uphill. On the streets of Santo Domingo unthreatening cops were emblazoned with names and numbers as prominent as those on a football jersey. By day, I discovered that library, parks, and schools are stitched together with new roads and footpaths, to enhance an impoverished but vibrant community.

The Jardin Botanico at the center of town has been spruced up. "Free admission; the mayoralty has already paid for you," reads a sign. The plantings have a tropical exuberance but the star attraction is the Orquideorama, a steel canopy that abstracts a grove of trees, and is faced in slats of wood. Ten hexagonal "trees" comprise six steel columns and ribs supporting a glass-covered space frame. At the base are orchid displays. The hexagons recur as slatted and closed elements in the flat roof. Mesh banners protect plants from excessive sun. The geometry complements the large trees and the structure spans a wide, lofty area. A bridal couple posed for photos in a period white convertible, children played tag around the planters, and families stopped to admire the blooms. [2010]

AYERS ROCK

More than 90 percent of Australians live in coastal cities and suburbs, shunning the vast, barren interior. Sydney and Melbourne are as sophisticated as any American city, with superior cuisine. That heightened my sense of adventure as I flew over a thousand miles of the Simpson Desert to Alice Springs, an outpost at the heart of the continent. From the air, the narrow strip of green morphed into an infinity of ochreous red, scored with dried stream beds, the white streaks of mineral deposits, and dunes that extend north-south for up to 200 miles. At the airport it was a cloudless 100 degrees. I rented a small car and drove as fast as I could for three hours, pausing at a truck stop for a lunch of kangaroo patties.

The land is flat, and Ayers Rock first appears as a blip on the horizon, gradually dominating the view like the mesas of the American southwest. Close-up it's as overwhelming and varied in its mass as is the void of the Grand Canyon. Its scars and screes are modeled by the harsh sun, and it's pierced by gorges and caves. To the Aboriginals, who call it Uluru, the rock is sacred and climbing will soon be prohibited. It's also a magnet for flies that cluster on one's face and are undeterred by insect repellent. Locals use veils and I was driven

to the same expedient. The best memento of that excursion was the Aboriginal painting I bought in Melbourne: a stylized map of waterholes linked by paths, all picked out in white dots, which had an odd resemblance to the desert seen from above. [2003]

Ayers Rock

HANOI

Driving in from the airport I was astonished to see how dramatically Vietnam's capital had expanded in the two decades since the government lifted its ban on private ownership. A city that was once a sleepy backwater has become vibrantly alive with a period mix of buildings inspired by Chinese and French models, a scatter of new commercial buildings, and a flourishing contemporary art scene. Narrow three-story houses with brightly painted facades, turrets, and lacy balconies are replacing the scatter of tin shacks and open-fronted workshops. Memories of the struggle for independence from the French, and of the American war are kept alive by the ruling communist party, which has preserved the body of Ho Chi Minh in a forbidding mausoleum, and enjoins its cadres to "Study and Follow Uncle Ho's Virtues," according to a headline in the English-language newspaper. But the people my friend Patrick Macrory and I met during our visit seemed intent on forgetting war and ideology, embracing capitalism with gusto, and welcoming Americans with broad smiles.

The cheerful chaos of the new suburbs subsided as our driver pulled up to the century-old Metropole. Every visitor of importance, from Charlie Chaplin to Somerset Maugham, Graham Greene, and Jane Fonda –stayed in this stately hotel, which has been restored and extended by Sofitel. Within the older guest rooms, with their hardwood floors, ceiling fans, and louvered shutters, little has changed. The bamboo bar opens onto the pool; the Art Deco wing is dazzlingly white. There are even solar topees set out on the chaises. It's a time capsule of the colonial past, and a calm retreat from the daily bustle.

Around the corner is the Opera, a provincial version of Charles Garnier's landmark in Paris, and it's surrounded by wide, tree-lined boulevards and the ochre villas of French colonial administrators, now government offices, and musty museums. Far more rewarding is the city's old quarter, a labyrinth of narrow streets, each named for one of 36 craft guilds and specializing in its products. The buildings are an anarchic jumble of Chinese, art nouveau, Art Deco, and modern. Stores sell tin boxes and counterfeit money (for offering to the dead), mirrors and gravestones, silks and bamboo ladders. Produce stalls fill the roadway, and the sidewalks are filled with shoppers and porters carrying baskets of fruit suspended from long poles. Here you can be fitted for a suit or dress and wear it that evening – though I found better choices in the old trading city of Hoi An, where tailoring is the principal activity. We ducked into the Memorial House Museum. Narrow and deep, it once housed a single merchant family in a warren of rooms that open onto two interior courtyards, and now offers a variety of arts and crafts for sale.

Many locals dine outdoors, bringing their own bowls to sample *pho,* the rice noodle and beef broth soup that is Vietnam's signature dish, and spooning up seasoned strips of grilled pork in *bun cha*, a local specialty. We lunched at Cha Ca Thang Long, a restaurant that

Bridge in Hoan Liem Lake, Hanoi

Rocks rising from Halong Bay

offers a single dish. A heaped plate of turmeric-flavored fish and fresh dill is brought to the table with a charcoal brazier for pan grilling. The waiter started us off and returned with more frosty Tiger beer. The simplicity and authenticity of the meal made a wonderful introduction to Vietnamese street food in a cool, quiet setting.

Relics of the past survived the destruction of war and revolution. The willow-shaded promenade around Hoan Kiem Lake is an outdoor stage for tai chi at first light and for strollers and chess players into the evening. An arched red bridge leads to the island temple of Den Ngoc Son, where carvings of frisky dragons bare their fangs and the preserved body of a giant turtle recalls an ancient legend. That and other popular tales are enacted at the Water Puppet Theater close by. Handlers standing chest-deep in a pool of water are concealed behind a decorative screen as they manipulate lions and unicorns, emperors and drunken boatmen. Peasants chase frogs, a boat race kicks up a storm, and fireworks explode in the finale.

A three-hour drive to the east from Hanoi is one of the natural wonders of the world: the UNESCO World Heritage site of Halong Bay. We rose at dawn to make an early start on a day trip that we could happily have stretched to two or three. Along the way, rice paddies with water buffalo and farmers in conical straw hats alternated with new developments, and a few traditional, straw-roofed huts. At 10 am the quay was lined with boats, each with a yellow dragon on its prow. Jagged rocks jutted from the still water and faded into the mist. There are 700 named islands in the bay and many more tiny peaks.

We cruised slowly around, passing junks with angular red sails, and floating markets where locals shop and tourists bargain for trinkets. A soft breeze cooled the upper deck and tugged at the canopy. The islands are full of caves. One of the most spectacular was a natural cathedral with stalactites for columns and a soaring roof vault. Lunch was served in the salon: cold crab and lobster in their shells, baked fish, and well-chilled Chablis. Back on deck, sleepy from the wine, we gazed into the watery world without end until, too soon, it was time to head back to shore. [2006]

INDIA

My second trip to India was done in style. Aman invited me to review their new hotel in Delhi, and comped me at their two country estates in Rajasthan. For a few days I was pampered like a British administrator in the days of Empire. A batman trailed me as I walked around, and a white SUV was ready to drive me wherever I wanted to go. It felt confining and I wanted to break out of the cocoon and enjoy the real India as I had 30 years before as a budget traveler.

I asked the driver to wait for me in the Old City, while I enjoyed a madcap dash around the main street of Chadni Chowk and the back alleys on a rickshaw. The driver fought off a rival for the privilege of taking me and urged me to brace my foot on the bracket supporting the saddle column. ("Your safety belt, dear sir," he said with a hearty laugh). The traffic zigged and zagged, with a succession of hairbreadth misses—thanks to innate survival skills—like fish swimming through water, or thanks to the gods (everyone has a little figure of Ganesh for luck). Grubby storefronts are plastered with signs in English and Hindi, promoting everything from eyeglasses to "fresh batches of income tax." There's an uninterrupted cacophony; a sign on the back of trucks reads "Horns Please"—as if anyone needed encouragement.

Delhi: Meliony flower market

The days passed rapidly. I made an early visit to the Meliony flower market where a street-full of stalls sell garlands of marigolds for religious offerings. Vendors stood around, chatting and drinking tea to ward off the dawn chill, or squatted on platforms – turbaned figures bathed in glow of single light bulbs like gods awaiting obeisance. The Qutub complex is a UNESCO World Heritage site where ruins of the first Indian mosque wrap around a 12th-century minaret of red sandstone flecked with green parrots. Hamayun's Tomb is a rough sketch for the Taj Mahal, but a century earlier and far simpler. It houses the remains of the second Mughal emperor, who died after tripping down the steep steps of a library while hurrying to a mosque. Subtly restored by the Aga Khan Trust, it preserves a sense of graceful decay in its pinkish-white dome with turrets around the base that glow softly in the late afternoon light.

There are many relics of the Raj, from St. Martin's garrison church, now a school chapel, to Edwin Lutyen's Viceroy's Palace, renamed the Rastrapati Bhavan and home to the Indian president. The grand staircase, vast ballroom, dining room, and other official spaces have a chilly grandeur, intended to intimidate and quite at odds with the spirit of a democratic

Qutub minaret in Delhi

Amanbagh: manicured lawns and white havelis

republic. Far more appealing is the Mughal-style garden, with its geometry of canals, crossed axes, and tiered sandstone fountains. Severely geometric gazebos to either side, and more gardens open off the first conveying the illusion of infinite boundaries. Two hundred gardeners maintain it in impeccable condition

It was a two-hour drive from the airport at Jaipur to Amanbagh. Brilliantly colored saris and turbans punctuated the arid landscape and the impoverished roadside settlements. Camels with supercilious upturned noses pulled huge loads, and a double line of women carried huge bundles of twigs on their heads. After two hours of negotiating the chaotic edge of the city and bumpy roads, the mirage of Amanbagh appeared: an otherworldly vision of

Itinerant musician from Jodhpur

manicured hedges, white havelis, a vast pool surrounded by a colonnade and bowling-green lawns. My suite had pink marble floors and a green marble bathroom. From this sybaritic oasis I took a jeep trip around the local villages in the late afternoon. Aman employs 80 percent of its staff from local villages, subsidizes the local school, and asks its staff to discourage their children from begging. That explains the innocence of small children who are content to smile and wave, asking nothing in return.

Boating on Lake Mansarova

Next day, I was driven out to Lake Mansarova, where still waters reflect mountains, for a tranquil voyage through this bird sanctuary. Two oarsmen and my escort sat in the rear, and I was given the center section, with its bowed canopy and gold silk gauze curtains supported on splayed red poles. I spotted black-headed ibis, Indian crane, egrets, cormorants, osprey, spoonbill, and a solitary pelican, while tucking into a tiffin of chick peas with pomegranate seeds, spicy vegetable rolls, herb and potato patties, and fruit salad. The silence was broken only by water dripping from the paddles, distant bird calls, and a muttered colloquy among the crew.

Aman-i-Khas had the feel of an encampment—a luxurious version of the tents that bearers erected for district officers on their travels. Sitting at a camp table writing up my notes in the evening, the birds and animals chorusing beyond, a chota peg to hand; the only differences from a hundred years ago are electricity, my laptop, and the fact that nobody dresses for dinner. The tent was almost as large as my apartment and twice as high in the middle, supported on four steel columns cleverly disguised with mirrors and closets. The bed in a curtained-off bay was flanked by a bath and a dressing room.

Dinner was served on the terrace: mulligatawny soup (lentils

A friendly neighbor of Amanbagh

Aman-i-Khas; Tiger in Rathambore National Park

and cocoanut milk; a far cry from the murky goo of my childhood), mild curried chicken, and delicious vegetables from the garden. A troupe of six musicians arrived, and started playing – wild sounds with haunting echoes of the central European folk music that inspired Bartók. There were links, through Sanskrit and wandering tribes, between northern India and Hungary. They came over to the fire pit, one by one, to demonstrate their instruments. One played a pair of pipes, which can sound like bagpipes, and a Jew's harp; another the drums; a sangari (which resembles a medieval viol); an accordion; a pottery bowl which can be tapped with a ring on the finger or blown into; and castanets. Another sang in harsh, plangent tones. They were from Jodhpur and travel around, performing at hotels and weddings.

I was woken at six next morning by the charwallah bringing coffee and toast, which he served on the screen porch while I showered in the dark and dressed. Wrapped up warmly I set off in a jeep with two Indians, and a couple from Edinburgh. Rathambore National Park was thronged with jeeps and open-top charabancs. Officially, they allow seven vehicles at a time in each of the five sectors, but a little baksheesh increases that number. For first hour, we encountered nothing but few spotted deer and peacock; then the driver glimpsed fresh spoor in the dust, the guide heard a warning cry and we were off. Another vehicle approached, and a tiger emerged from the brush and strolled nonchalantly along the path between us, as unhurriedly as a domestic cat patrolling one's house. I was close enough to reach out and stroke it. Wisely, I refrained. Five other vehicles joined the first and I wondered if guides had figured out a way to communicate with each other, since a good sighting boosts their tips – as our driver was happy to tell us.

Jantar Mantal in Jaipur

From Aman-i-Khas I returned to Jaipur to see the Hawa Mahal, a palatial facade with fretted openings and gold pinnacles. Jantar Mantar is an 18th-century observatory that's even more ambitious and impeccably maintained than the one in Delhi. Its abstract sculptural forms were precisely calibrated instruments, used by court astrologers to forecast the alignment of the planets. They are proto-modern: a good example of science getting out ahead of art, of functionalism generating beauty.

Early the next day a hired car took me to Shekwati, a region north of Jaipur that was built up by merchants whose descendants have now moved away, leaving many family mansions shuttered and abandoned. Every wall is frescoed with elephants, horses, and feudal imagery, alternating with naïve portraits of contemporary life. There's a train, painted by someone who had obviously never seen one. Each passenger sits separately, as though in a palanquin on wheels. Elsewhere, there are early flying machines, cars, and lines of British soldiers, marching stiffly.

Darkness fell as we reached the industrial fringe of Jaipur, 15 miles from the center. The city's population has grown to six million, and every one of them seems to be fighting for dominance or a right of way on the road into the city. Anyone can get a license by paying 200 rupees – even a blind man my driver remarked. The result is a kind of death race, with overloaded trucks hogging the fast lanes, and auto-rickshaws, jitneys, motorbikes, cyclists, small vans, and everything else on wheels competing for the rest. [2009]

Hawa Mahal, Jaipur

Frescoes in Shekwati

SINGAPORE

Shophouses and a Chinese temple (now the Amoy Hotel) on Telok Ayer Street

Descending into Singapore I looked down on a natural harbor thronged with freighters waiting to unload and a wall of apartment towers rising from the shore. The airport terminal was carpeted and squeaky clean; the freeway to downtown was flanked with tropical vegetation. The image of this city-state is established at the outset: a fusion of Swiss order and Chinese energy, prosperous and green.

The contrasts are immediately apparent. Steel and glass office towers loom over rows of three-story shophouses from the colonial era. Chinatown, Little India, and Arab Street abut the international financial district. The cuisine is equally varied, and one of the great treats is to sample local specialities in one of the many hawkers' centers--Maxwell being one of the best. Singaporeans live to eat and that provides an incentive for the humblest stall. Other Asian cities are jammed with traffic; here, car ownership is restricted by heavy taxes and the entire island is tied together by a network of fast, spotless subway trains. Infill has greatly increased the size of the island, and the goverment owns all the land, commissioning subsidized apartment towers, leasing plots for commercial development, and insisting on a generous provision of greenery--from urban terraces to a surviving patch of rain forest.

I spent a week with my friend Lauree exploring inventive new buildings by local practitioners and some of the world's most celebrated architects. Standouts included Marina One: Ingenhoven Architects' mixed-use development, which occupies an entire city block. Four wavy towers, linked by mesh sunshades, undulate around a multilevel courtyard that's as lushly planted as the Botanical Gardens or the waterfront conservatories. Stylized waterfalls splash into pools, and ramps ascend to shops and restaurants, upper-level offices and apartments.

The Interlace is a residential complex of 31 six-storey bars of apartments, piled atop each other to enclose hexagonal courtyards. A resident gave us a private tour of Ole Scheeren's masterpiece, where a thousand families enjoy a balance of privacy and community, pools and playgrounds, just ten minutes from downtown. Students are the principal users of Thomas Heatherwick's Hive, a cluster of richly textured concrete cylinders ranged around

Looking up from the courtyard of Marina One

a ten-storey atrium at the National Technological University. Glass-fronted classrooms open onto galleries and curved balconies at each level, offering flexibility within and social interaction without.

The local firm of WOHA has created a succession of environmentally responsive buildings over the past two decades. We stayed at their Oasia Downtown hotel, a tower clad in red metal mesh that serves as a climbing frame for plants, and spent a day touring other recent work. Their School of the Arts has a cavernous base of striated concrete that evokes a rock canyon and serves as a public gathering space, with auditoria that are rented out for events. Above are six levels of classrooms surrounding an atrium, linked by a spiral stair as tightly wound as a spring. On the street it was 85 degrees and humid, for Singapore is just above the Equator; in SOTA the architects channel breezes through strategically placed openings to lower the temperature by at least 10 degrees.

We walked through the Enabling Village, a low-budget conversion of a technical school that serves as a rehabilitation center for the handicapped. Visitors are welcome to explore this joyful community, with its lively facades and scavenged materials, from concrete sewer pipes to cut-up shipping containers that serve as garden pavilions. We ended the tour at the Stadium MRT (underground railway) station, which has to accomodate the crowds attending a major sports complex. Within a simple canopy is another canyon reaching deep into the ground and accessed by long escalators. Windows at either end are etched with leaping football players, and the platform below is paved in blue and green terrazzo, marked with arrows to direct passengers in and out of the trains. Everything is clearly signposted, and friendly English-speaking staff are on hand to answer questions. As an American, familiar with the New York subway and the shortage of public transit in most cities, I felt like a refugee from an underdeveloped country.

The Hive at the National Technology University

The Interlace apartment complex

We spent a night in the Amoy, a boutique hotel created within the shell of the first Chinese temple on the island. Dinner treats included Candlenut, a Michelin-starred restaurant in an old army barracks on Dempsey Road; Zam Zam, a frugal restaurant in the Moslem quarter, across from a gold-domed mosque; and Bam!, a Japanese restaurant on Tras Street serving a pricey but delicious prix fixe. One night, friends took us for cocktails to the Polo Club (a popular relic of British rule), and dinner at Hua Yu Wee on Upper East Coast Road, which was packed to capacity with Chinese families on the eve of their New Year. The feast began with a special holiday salad, tossed high with loud toasts to bring good luck and mix the varied flavors; crab and sharks fin soup, deep fried tofu, sauteed squid, and rock lobsters. Sadly we missed Folklore at the Destination Singapore Beach Road Hotel, where chef Damian D'Silva serves heritage dishes to an eager following. [2018]

Stadium MRT station and (right) Maxwell Hawkers' Center

ITALY: APULIA

Castel del Monte; Trani Cathedral

Apulia is a surprisingly fertile province in the heel of Italy – in sharp contrast to the barren toe. I followed the trail of the Norman knights who settled here a thousand years ago, exploring their castles and cathedrals, and lingering in towns that seem to have migrated from an island in the Aegean. The sunlight is as brilliant as that of Greece and, away from the port cities of Bari and Brindisi, it's farm country. Tourists are bused in to see the clustered trulli of Alborobello, which markets itself as a kind of Hobbitsville, but few stay to explore the monuments.

The greatest of these is Castel del Monte. An octagonal block with octagonal towers at each corner, it rises from a hill to dominate the countryside around. Too remote to be a defensive position and too cramped to be a hunting lodge, it may have been constructed as a symbol of authority by Frederick II, the ruler who was called *stupor mundi*, the wonder of the world. For centuries it was a ruin, abandoned and used as a quarry; now the exterior has been refaced with pale stone, and it's probably as crisp today as when it was completed around 1250.

Almost as impressive is the Romanesque cathedral that looms over the waterfront of Trani. Eroded lions, griffons, and elephants jut from the sheer west front and the three rounded apses are as stark as grain silos. The stone of the walls and piazza have the sheen of a sea-washed pebble. It's hard to believe that this vast pile was built in a small town, and that its expressive simplicity is eight centuries old. It was meant to offer protection, so the windows are small and mostly high up. That gives the bare interiors a sense of mystery as sunlight filters down among the massive columns as though through the trees in a forest.

Locorotondo is a compact hill town, gleaming white and well maintained. Ostuni is even more compelling: a maze of white houses, steps and switchback ramps that pivot around two honey-toned churches, one baroque, one Gothic; both extravagant. In the blaze of midday the whiteness was as dazzling as that of Mykonos. There was a murmur

Stepped street, Ostuni

of voices from within the shuttered houses at this hour of lunch and siesta; later, the doors would open and the residents would emerge to sit on stoops and in alleyways too narrow for cars. From the ramparts, the views were as sweeping as those from the castles, with fields and scattered farms extending away to the Adriatic.

From here I drove south to Lecce, a city that's as exuberant as the Norman buildings are austere. The churches in the historic center—Santa Croce, San Giovanni Battista, San Matteo, and the cathedral— are triumphs of ornament, thanks to the abundance of soft golden sandstone. Lecce was a prosperous backwater of the Spanish empire during the baroque era, and nobles competed to flaunt their wealth and enrich the city. It went into a long decline and has now been meticulously restored and made a pedestrian zone. [1989]

Memento mori, Bitonto

PALLADIANA

Driving around the Veneto in the rain on truck-clogged roads is a chore, but the villas of Palladio justify the ordeal. Using a house near Venice as a base, I spent a week marveling at the versatility of an architect who has inspired so many generations over the past four centuries. A succession of serendipitous encounters brought these frescoed halls alive. Niccolò Valmarana showed me around the Villa Rotunda, the masterpiece his ancestors commissioned. We climbed a narrow spiral stair to a wooden gallery from where the entire dome appears like a painted stage set – as thrilling as the same architect's Teatro Olimpico.

At the Villa Marcello, I had an introduction to the owner. I rang the doorbell and was met by his cousin, Count Girolamo Marcello, a spry octogenarian. He welcomed me as though I were an old chum, and gave me a tour of the house, instructing his teenage great nephews to open the shutters. Gray light threw the stucco moldings into sharp relief, and revealed the frescoes of G. B. Crosato—a rival of G. B. Tiepolo—in the galleried ballroom. One of the grandest of these country estates is the Villa Emo, with its iconic portico, a green axis extending to the hills in back, and trompe l'oeil frescoes. A barn full of traditional agricultural implements is a reminder that these villas were part of working farms. On a later visit I was lucky enough to see it in a late-afternoon glow that enhanced its timeless beauty. Caroline Emo, the Count's ex-wife, was there and we sat out in the portico and chatted for an hour about the architecture and the challenge of maintaining a house as large and fragile as this.

Ferrari rally in the Piazza dei Signori of Vicenza

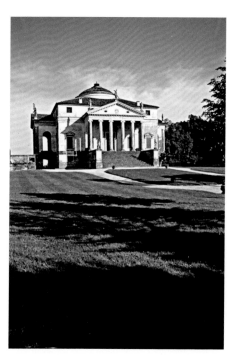

Vicenza: Villa Rotunda

I spent a day in Vicenza, Palladio's hometown, revisiting his basilica, theater, and palaces.

Early next morning I went to Piazza dei Signori and found it full of red Ferraris, which had driven here from all over Europe for a rally. Proud owners gave them a final polish before climbing inside. As the clock struck nine, they revved up in unison, filling the square with an almighty roar and, one by one, sped away.

There were disappointments. Some villas have become institutionalized and have lost their soul, while others are crumbling into dust. I remembered an excursion to the Villa Barbaro at Maser in the 1960s, when visitors were few and were allowed to wander through the staterooms, admiring the Veronese frescoes. Now, the best rooms were locked and the remaining frescoes were obscured behind pots of wilting lilies. The magic had fled. [1990]

MODERNIST HEYDAY

The 1930s marked a high point in Italian architecture, but, for left-leaning designers and academics, everything built at that time is tainted by its link to fascism. It's a foolish prejudice. The regime embraced modernism as a symbol of the new Italy, even as the Nazis and Soviets retreated into leaden pastiche, and condemned progressive architecture as Bolshevik or bourgeois. Nine decades after Mussolini overruled reactionaries and insisted on a contemporary station for Florence, it's time for a reappraisal of that decade.

Much as I love the rich legacy of Italian architecture and urbanism, from ancient Rome to the Renaissance, I prefer to make discoveries, especially buildings that are ignored or condemned by the mainstream. I smile at the bombastic inscriptions and mock-heroic statuary of the Foro Mussolini in Rome, and other official sites. As in any era, good and bad, pompous and elegant co-existed; it's essential to make distinctions. Giuseppi Terragni's masterpiece is the Casa del Fascio in Como: once a den of blackshirts and inflammatory rhetoric, now a police station that strives to serve the community. The toxic ideology of that era has largely vanished, the monuments endure, just as the Coliseum has long outlived the cruelty of gladiatorial combat.

Terragni, though a committed fascist through his 20-year career, has been rehabilitated, and Como has become a place of pilgrimage – for his kindergarten, Novocommun apartments, war memorial, and villas as well as the Casa del Fascio. What might he have achieved had he not died in 1941. Other architects were politically neutral or opportunistic; they went where the work was. The regime knew how to get things done. Schools, post-offices, city halls, and sports facilities are models of creative design and quality construction--in the homeland and possessions as far removed as Asmara in Eritrea, and Istria (see Angiolo Mazzoni's post office in Pula). The new town of Sabaudia, one of several that marked the draining of the Pontine marches south of Rome, was "built by warriors in 253 days," as an inscription proclaims. Pure propaganda, of course, but so ambitious a development is unimaginable in present-day Italy where a single building can fall victim to bureaucratic foot-dragging, cost-cutting, shoddy construction, and cost-overruns.

Casa del Fascio, Como; Palazzo della Civiltà in the EUR district of Rome

Repurposed holiday camp in Catolica on the Adriatic coast

In Florence, not one visitor in a thousand notices Angioli Mazzoni's Centrale Termica, the power plant beside the station, which now stands empty and disfigured with graffiti. It's a heroic expression of Futurism, and its muscularity and bold modeling have a strong affinity to Russian Constructivism. It cries out to be restored and given a new role: perhaps as a museum of architecture, or of the industries and crafts that made Florence so prosperous. Other modernist treasures are scattered around the city, but the highlight is rarely accessible: the Scuola di Guerra Aerea, which is still an air force school. It was a prestige commission of 1937, designed by the Florentine architect Raffaelo Fagnoni, and completed in less than a year. The beauty and refinement of these low-rise brick blocks, widely spaced and well-landscaped, gives them a timeless quality. Gray glass mosaics, a suspended staircase, and original custom furnishings survived the devastating flood of 1966.

The paternalism of the regime and leading corporations found expression in workers' holiday camps, and there was a special emphasis on youth. A few of these—Colonia Maritima was the generic name—survive intact. In Catolica, south of Rimini, an aquarium occupies dormitories that resemble ships' hulls, with rounded metallic ends and porthole windows. A much grander example in Calambrone, west of Pisa, has been rehabilitated to serve as a popular beach resort. Originally it was named Colonia Rosa Maltoni Mussolini, for Il Duce's mother, and it was designed by Giuseppe Mazzini for families of railway and telegraph employees. Two cylindrical towers wrapped with staircases complement a low-rise arc of dormitory buildings, a columned entry pavilion, and a succession of crisply detailed blocks of guest rooms and a dining hall, all clad in terracotta-toned stucco. Ask nicely and they'll let you walk around.

Olivetti turned Ivrea, northwest of Turin, into a model company town from the 1930s on, and other corporations followed suit. But the 1930s is a demonstration of how enlightened and effective government can be – in Italy of that decade as in the PWA programs of the American New Deal. There's a pressing need to protect, re-animate, and chronicle the best of this epoch, before even more of it crumbles away. [1989/2017]

A workers' resort in Calambrone, west of Pisa, is now a beach hotel

Casa Malaparte; Staircase to roof terrace

CASA MALAPARTE

The sea was choppy as I set off in a small boat from the port of Capri to have lunch at the Casa Malaparte on the southern tip of the island. The sirens no longer lure mariners to destruction on the rocky shores of the island but the wilder parts still look as they did in classical times. Curzio Malaparte, an Italian writer, was brought to Point Massullo at Christmas 1937, and immediately decided to build on a site where "nature expresses itself with incomparable force and cruelty. It is a place suited to brave men and free spirits."

He commissioned a design from a young architect, Adalberto Libera, rejected it as too conventional, and decided to create a self-portrait—the *Casa Come Me*—with help from a local builder. A two-story block perches on a rocky spur high above sea. Steps lead down to a landing stage and there I alighted to join Niccolò Rositani, nephew of the writer, who had driven his Maserati down from Florence that morning.

Few houses have cast such a spell over architects, and its distinctive profile has echoed down the years. The rock walls are clad in red-toned stucco, recalling the Tuscan farmhouses of the writer's childhood. A kitchen and small guest rooms occupy the lower floor. Malaparte entertained in the grand salon upstairs and wrote for 30 years in the study at the far end. In a novel he imagines that Field Marshal Rommel came here during the German occupation and asked if he was the

Living room windows frame views of the rocky coast

architect. "No, but I designed the scenery," he declared, waving his arm towards the deep-set windows that frame views of rocks and distant shores.

The signature feature is the wedge of brick-clad steps that ascend, like those on a sacrificial altar, to an unrailed roof terrace. In Jean-Luc Godard's *Contempt*, Brigitte Bardot sunbathes in the nude on this very spot; sadly, it was empty when I went up, but the feeling of hovering above the sea was compelling. Malaparte swung from far right to far left in his politics and he was exiled for two years to Lipari. He borrowed the wedge of stairs from the Annunziata church on that barren island. In his final years, Mao invited him to China, where he contracted a fatal illness, in spite of which he bequeathed the house to the communist regime, which had no use for it. Fortunately, they were willing to give it up. Niccolò and his wife, Alessia Suckert, head the foundation that maintains the house, protecting it from the elements and hosting scholarly symposia. [1994]

ROME

Visiting Rome, it's easy to empathize with the gladiators, though traffic and tour groups have replaced lions as the foe. Of course, it's worth the fight. The rewards of this palimpsest of history are still immense, and everyone has a favorite monument, piazza, or fountain. There are surprises around every corner. I once encountered a band of stilt walkers, entirely self absorbed and drawing no attention from passers-by. The funniest site is the Foro Mussolini, a mock classical stadium built in anticipation of the 1940 Olympics (which were canceled at the outbreak of war). White-marble statues of nude athletes symbolize the cities of Italy. Some have acquired fig leaves, some not, and I wonder whether the choice was left to local watch committees. One can imagine a delegation of ladies from Livorno putting up a step-ladder and gluing a patch over the offending private parts, while tut-tutting about the failure of their sisters in Pisa to observe the proprieties.

One evening I discovered another entertaining spectacle at the Villa Medici, which has housed the French Academy since 1803. For most of its history, budding artists came here to study antiquity, but the curriculum was updated in 1968, and the plaster casts were relegated to the garden. There, they form a tragic tableaux vigorously protesting their exile.

Equally surprising is the Centrale Montemartini, a power station of 1912 that has been decommissioned but retains its immense turbines. In 1997 it was pressed into service as a temporary exhibition space while the Capitoline Museum was under restoration, and proved so popular that its term has been extended indefinitely. Roman sculptures are lined up against the black steel boilers, contradicting Marinetti who wrote, in the 1909 Futurist Manifesto, that the machine in all its brutish glory was more beautiful than the Winged Victory of Samothrace. Here it's a tie; classical and modern play off each other, and each seems more beautiful as a result of the juxtaposition. [2002]

Abandoned plaster casts at the Villa Medici

Rome: Foro Mussolini

TURIN

Best known as Italy's Detroit, Turin is a treasury of unique architecture, from the baroque churches of Guarino Guarini to the Mole Antonelliana, a towering synagogue turned movie museum, and Lingotto, the former Fiat factory with its rooftop test track. But the ghost one keeps encountering is that of Carlo Mollino (1905–73), a flamboyant contemporary of Gio Ponti – and almost as versatile. He designed houses and a riding club, rebuilt the Teatro Reggio, and created eccentric chairs and tables that go for astronomical prices at auction. He also found time for erotic photography, downhill skiing, and racing cars.

The Casa Mollino is run as a private foundation by family members, one of whom guided me around. Mollino never lived here—he had four other houses—and he furnished this apartment in 1968 as a self-portrait and a surreal work of art that blends personal references with inherited

Carlo Mollino's apartment in Turin

furniture. After his death an engineer lived here, and the apartment had to be restored to its original state, based on Mollino's detailed plan.

A vintage milking stool stands next to the thin-backed white chair it inspired. The dining room has an oval table supported on fluted classical columns, surrounded with Eero Saarinen's tulip chairs. A German forest engraving frames classical doors. The bed is in the form of an Egyptian boat with mystical signs that indicate a voyage into world of dead. Velvet curtains can be drawn to close off each room. Claustrophobic and exhilarating by turns, the apartment is the embodiment of decadence and the free spirit of a true original. [2009]

GIO PONTI

Architect, designer, artist, and founding editor of *Domus* – Gio Ponti (1891–1975) was a Renaissance man for our own times. I have had the good fortune to explore his houses and churches in Milan, stay in the shadow of his Pirelli tower, and sit on his Superleggera chair. Highlights of a recent trip to Italy were his interiors for an ancient university and a cool modern hotel.

The University of Padua was established in 1222 by students from Bologna and everyone of importance seems to have taught there, from Dante to Copernicus and Galileo, drawn by its tradition of tolerance. Today, there are 60,000 students, giving it a commanding presence in a city of 200,000. In 1939, a courtyard of the Palazzo Bo was remodeled and Ponti was

Gio Ponti's Senior Common Room for the University of Padua

Lobby of the Parco dei Principi Hotel, Sorrento

119

commissioned to design the frescoes on the staircase leading up to the rector's office, and the furnishings of the adjoining rooms. The project was realized in a curious mix of crafted wood, brilliant details, and the occasional rhetorical flourish. The basilica, a hall with dark red columns, is especially impressive, as is the striped terrazzo floor in the senior common room. Every piece of furniture was custom designed, down to the bronze door handles. Concurrently, Ponti designed the Palazzo Liviano, a building for the art department a few blocks away. In its museum, plaster casts of antique sculptures are displayed within serried yellow walls and an Apollo occupies a Pompeian red niche.

The Hotel Parco Dei Principi, is a 96-room jewel perched high on a rocky escarpment, looking across the Bay of Naples to Vesuvius. Ponti designed it in 1962, next to a neo-classical villa that had been owned by the Tsar's cousin. A marker on the checkered terrace shows where a dancer from the Imperial Theater in St. Petersburg performed.

You wind through a lush sub-tropical garden to the expansive lobby, and through glass doors to the dining room and terrace. Beyond is the bar, villa, and an irregular, stepped pool. Inspired by the blue of sea and sky, Ponti used that color throughout, on tiled "rugs" of simple geometries on a white ground; blue and white pebbles on bar and kiosk walls; as well as a diversity of hand-painted and modeled tiles on columns. Every guest room has a different floor pattern, complementing the original blond-wood cabinets and tables. Chairs are upholstered in blue wool. It may sound monotonous but the effect is intoxicating: a total immersion in one tone that lifts one's spirits heavenwards. As Monet wrote from Antibes during his first trip to the Mediterranean in 1884: "One swims in blue air; it is frightening." [2017]

SWITZERLAND: ZURICH

Ulli Zollikofer was a Zuricher whose exuberance, generosity, and iconoclasm brought his staid city alive. He lived well, traveled constantly, and drove insanely fast before he was felled by a stroke. One spring I was staying at his house on the lake when a friend called to say his ad agency had won a top national prize. We were both invited to the celebration at Irene's Cuisine, a cookery school 20 miles out of the city.

A score of urban sophisticates, impeccably dressed, donned aprons and were put to work cooking our five-course dinner. Irene played ringmaster, cracking her metaphorical whip, urging us to chop, dice, peel, puree, and stuff. The women knew just what to do and I watched in horrified fascination as one beauty in a white satin dress picked up a succession of chicken breasts and split them, pulling a razor-sharp knife towards her palm. I nicked my finger and asked Irene, "Haben Sie ein band-aid, bitte?" Unfazed she opened a drawer and pulled out a roll of plaster that would have staunched the bleeding of a severed arm. She paused to demonstrate a few complicated techniques and cheered us on as though we were her students. Wine flowed freely, there were no life-threatening accidents, and the dinner would have won us at least one Michelin star. Around midnight, Irene drew a map to indicate which roads might have police traps, and we sped back to the city. [1990]

APPELZELL

Voters gather in the town square of Appenzell

The canton of Appenzell is picture book Switzerland, with its gaily-painted facades, charming folk customs, and direct democracy. Just what Orson Welles extolled in *The Third Man*. On the last Sunday of April voters gather in the town square for the *Landesgemeine*, an assembly that elects officials and approves laws. I was there for the last all-male gathering and the square was filled to capacity with electors in their best Sunday suits, each carrying a ceremonial sword or dagger. Some had walked for miles from scattered farms. Costumed marshals waving flags flanked the officers and magistrates who marched slowly to a dais, led by the town band. Votes were taken by a show of hands and at the end, the measure to give women the vote was defeated.

I left early for lunch to beat the crowd and found a pub full of women watching the proceedings on television. All eyes swiveled to the enemy, though, lacking side arms, I was clearly no more than a spectator. One can imagine the husbands who followed me in receiving a very cold reception. Later that year, two women appealed to the Federal Court and Appenzell was compelled to grant female suffrage – the last canton to do so. [1990]

FRANCE: PARIS SHOPS

A book on Paris was conceived on the rear platform of a number 29 bus, barreling down the Rue des Francs-Bourgeois in the Marais. Its route, from the Gare St. Lazare to the Bastille and beyond, is tortuous, so the driver is usually running behind schedule and puts on speed along this straight stretch. It was evening, and each shop window we passed suggested a miniature theater stage: its décor brightly lit, its mannequins like actors in frozen poses. We, the audience, were rushing by, and I wanted to get off and admire each tableau. But the shops were closed and it was the last night of my stay. So I returned the following year to chronicle the beauty of carved and painted window frames, the play of light and reflections off the glass, artistic displays, and abundant surprises back-stage.

My plan was to shoot the windows from the street and have a professional photograph the interiors. At the last moment she dropped out and persuaded me to do the whole job myself. Deeply apprehensive, I carried my tripod into the first shop on my list and asked

The late Lionel Poilâne in his bakery

if I might take some pictures. Would my fractured French convince them I was there to celebrate beauty not to case the joint? Would they mind if I browsed and bought nothing? The assistant called the owner; permission was granted and I was on my way.

Over the next four weeks I explored emporia of every kind. I was invited to see the medieval ovens of Poilâne, a legendary baker, and to sample the rum baba invented in 1725 by the founder of the Stohrer patisserie. The manager of Barthélmy instructed me on the art of ageing cheeses, Mme. Gély unfurled her vintage umbrellas and the owners of La Tuile à Loup unpacked pottery they had sourced from every corner of France. André Bissonnet played a hurdy gurdy in a store that was filled to bursting point with vintage instruments. And I trod the creaky floors of Déyrolle, since ravaged by fire, to marvel at their menagerie of stuffed animals. Some stores have the tranquility of the Musée Carnavalet. At La Maison de Poupée, a cat snoozed in an open drawer, and the owner sat, as still and porcelain-pretty as one of her dolls in a room where the loudest sound was the ticking of an old clock.

The passion of the shopkeepers I met was as engaging as the spectacle. They are skilled in the art of arrangement and doing simple things well. Defiantly individualistic, they have held the franchise tide at bay, preferring to sell a few choice items to a handful of dedicated customers. Occasionally, there were setbacks. Warren (she uses only one name) turns dried

Parisian patisserie

flowers into hats and was initially hesitant to let me photograph them. A Japanese crew had invaded her store the previous year, documented every piece, and opened a facsimile boutique in Tokyo. I explained that my hat-making skills were limited, so I was no threat, and that the Japanese lacked her powers of invention and would soon run out of steam. I photographed the 18th-century facade of Ladurée, the chic tearoom on the rue Royale. A member of staff ran towards me accusing me of sneaking a shot from the sidewalk and—discovering I was born in England (which was currently afflicted with mad cow disease)—screamed *vache folle! vache folle!* while doing a little war dance. It seemed a small annoyance amid so many rewarding encounters.

Some of the boutiques must have closed since I wrote the book, and I wonder how many of these specialists will survive rising rents and on-line shopping. Just before my book went to press, the owner of L'Encre Violette, a shop in the Marais that sold writing supplies, sent a hand-written note in purple ink. "The little authentic boutiques that gave certain quarters their charm are closing, one after another," she wrote, "Paris is losing its identity. There you have it: the end of a beautiful and sad story." [1999]

André Bissonnet with his instroments (right) Mme Gély shows her umbrellas

DÉSERT DE RETZ

Painted Tartar tent in the Désert de Retz

One of my best friends in Paris, sadly deceased, was Sir Valentine Abdy Bt., who survived a near-fatal car crash as a child, lived a rewarding life as an art connoisseur, and seemed to know everyone who mattered. Though hobbled from the accident, he had a fondness for fast cars, and we took several hair-raising drives around the Île de France with time out for bucolic lunches in a riverside inn that Renoir might have painted.

He was the ideal companion for an exploration of the Désert de Retz, a legendary landscape garden in the forest of Marly, twelve miles west of Paris but infinitely far in spirit. It was created on the eve of the French Revolution by the chevalier François Racine de Monville, a rich and romantic dilettante. When the King reproached his latest amour for sleeping with de Monville, she made the excuse, "but, Sire, he has such a handsome leg." Miraculously he survived the Terror after being arrested on a charge of sybaritism. He died at home in 1797, reputedly in the arms of his young mistress.

As a refuge from Versailles, the garden was popular with royals and courtiers. Marie Antoinette was inspired to create her rustic hamlet, Gustav III of Sweden found a model for his country retreat at Drottingholm, and Louis XVI, an unwilling captive of protocol, must have paid a visit. They entered from the forest, through a grotto guarded by statues of satyrs holding flaming torches. Within de Monville's hundred acres they found a three-dimensional recreation of a Hubert Robert landscape with ruins: an obelisk, an icehouse in the form of a pyramid, a Temple of Pan, and a classical theater. There was a ruined Gothic church, a fanciful Chinese house, and a painted Tartar tent that occupied an island.

Towering above these follies was a 75-foot-high broken column with four stories of rooms opening off a spiral stair. Thomas Jefferson—then the American Minister to France—borrowed its floor plan in his unrealized design for the US Capitol. After a long period of neglect, the Désert was being restored, and we found it conveniently close to another renewed masterwork, Le Corbusier's Villa Savoie. [1991]

VERSAILLES FOUNTAINS

Jets of water rise from manicured parterres to the sound of trumpets and kettledrums. Clouds of spray envelop stone goddesses, splash over balustrades, and dissolve the geometry of hedges and walkways. It's Sunday in the gardens of the Palace of Versailles, and the fountains are playing. *Les Grandes Eaux Musicales* as this spectacle is known, was originally reserved for the King of France – one of his many pleasurable escapes from the gilded prison of the palace. Now it's reprised for summer visitors: a brief preview in the late morning and a sustained burst of activity in the middle of the afternoon.

Les Grandes Eaux Musicales

I came for the overture, then rented a bicycle to ride along the shady drives of the park to the Petit Trianon – another escape hatch for the king and his mistresses. A leisurely lunch beside the Grand Canal then back, to return the bike, and prepare for a 90-minute trek around a score of fountains in the formal gardens. Some are spectacular, others are well concealed, but each is *vaut le voyage*, so it helps to have a map. Two great basins mark the central axis, and jets spout from dolphins and naiads flanking the sculptural wedding cakes that are crowded with gods and Apollo in his chariot. Water cascades over the rocks of a circular theater and glistens off the black grapes and gilded body of Bacchus, shimmering in the sunlight. Rameau's stately court music plays from speakers concealed in the bushes. I closed my eyes and imagined Louis XVI and Marie Antoinette taking a last stroll in this watery wonderland before the mob carried them off to Paris. [1996]

CAFÉ AUBETTE

One of the boldest art movements of the 1920s was De Stijl, the response of a group of Dutch artists and architects to the destruction of the First World War and the overthrow of traditional values. The most celebrated achievements of this movement are Gerrit Rietveld's blue and red chair and his iconoclastic villa for Truss Schröder in Utrecht. Almost forgotten is the Café Aubette, named for an 18th-century palace on the Place Kléber in Strasbourg. I climbed a broad flight of steps within this echoing pile, found my host at the door, stepped inside, and felt as disoriented as Alice tumbling down the rabbit hole.

Angled planes of color rose from bands of silver running diagonally across the walls and ceiling. Suspended rods supported two rows of uplights parallel to a long gallery. Booths flanked a parquet floor and a movie screen. In 1928 you might have come to gape at this daring artistic experiment and kick up your heels to the wail of a sax and the percussive rhythms of *le jazz hot*. Tall windows frame views of the square. There it is still the 19th century; within it's a ferment of modernism created by Theo van Doesberg, Jean Arp, and Sophie Taueber-Arp. Long abandoned, the restoration was underway during my visit. Dutch experts drew on the artists' colored sketches, original black and white photography, and paint samples. Ironically, much of the original décor survived because it was covered up soon after completion in response to customers' complaints.[2006]

Restored interior of the Café Aubette

VILLA E.1027

Artists—from Monet to Matisse—led the way in discovering the natural beauty of the French Riviera, celebrating its vibrant colors and brilliant light in their paintings. Eileen Gray, an Irish artist turned designer with a successful practice in Paris, fell in love with the rocky slopes of Cap Martin, overlooking the Mediterranean, and in 1925 bought a plot of land. Over the next three years, she designed and built a legendary white villa for her mentor, the Romanian architect Jean Badovici. He was part of the Parisian avant-garde and edited the progressive journal *L'Architecture Vivante*. She named the house E.1027, code for her initials and his.

A visionary designer and intuitive architect, Gray (1878–1976) created a total work of art. Though modest in scale, it embodies the spirit of its era, and the brilliance of a woman who has posthumously achieved the recognition she was long denied. Now, as then, you reach E.1027 along a path that leads from the coastal railroad station of Roquebrune. Gray—who always cherished privacy—preserved the terraces of a former lemon grove so that you glimpse the house only as you descend. In the 1950s, Le Corbusier added camping units, a restaurant—L'Etoile de Mer—and Le Cabanon, an artfully planned cabin where he spent the summers until 1965, when he drowned while swimming at the beach below. He and his wife are buried in the cemetery of Rocquebrune, high above.

"External architecture seems to have absorbed avant-garde architects at the expense of the interior, as if a house should be conceived for the pleasure of the eye more than for the well-being of its inhabitants," wrote Gray, in a jab at the great modern form givers. "A house is not a machine to live in ... Not only its visual harmony but its entire organization, all the terms of the work, combine to render it human in the most profound sense."

Eileen Gray furnished E. 1027 as a total work of art

There's wit in abundance, along with meticulous planning and a love of surprise. The house is oriented to the path of the sun, and louvered shutters open and tilt to provide shade and cross ventilation. The indoor-outdoor kitchen is set apart in the traditional rural way to keep cooking odors from entering the living areas. From the entry you can take different routes and an elliptical storage cabinet defines a foyer. Gray's bedroom adjoins the expansive living room, which opens onto the terrace through folding glass doors. Sailcloth awnings shelter the terrace and a suspended lifebelt plays up the nautical references, as do the splashes of blue on the pilotis and within. Stenciled messages enjoin visitors to "enter slowly" and "not to laugh."

Furniture, rugs and colored tile floors demarcate zones for sitting, resting, washing, and working. Built-in storage units with pivoting drawers are an extension of the architecture. Lightweight tables of steel and glass can easily be moved onto the terrace, or adjusted in height. Chairs include the classic Bibendum (named for the Michelin man) and the Transat (which was inspired by the deck chairs on transatlantic liners). Zeev Aram, whose London-based firm has reissued many Gray classics, donated replacements for the originals, which were sold or stolen decades ago.

The elephant in the room was put there by Le Corbusier when he returned in 1939, telling Badovici that he had "a furious desire to dirty the walls." Eight lurid murals destroy the harmony of Gray's compositions. She was outraged and never returned. The murals were conserved after wartime damage and acquired an importance of their own. Ironically, their presence may have saved the house from destruction. [2015]

VILLA CAVROIX

The Villa Cavroix, one of the greatest houses of the 20th century, is located near the battlefields of northeastern France and it survived two near-death experiences. Created in 1930–32 by Robert Mallet-Stevens (1886–1945) for the family of a textile magnate, it was vandalized by the Nazis, who used it as a barracks, and later by a developer who wanted to replace it with tract housing. Preservationists compared it to a sinking liner and

Villa Cavroix from the garden

there seemed little hope of rescue until, in 2001, it was bought by the State, given a $25 million restoration, and opened to the public.

In photographs, Mallet Stevens appears lean and tanned with a hawk-like profile, fastidiously dressed as though he had designed himself. Progressive from the start, he studied architecture at an advanced school, immersed himself in the European avant-garde, and volunteered as a pilot in the first World War. In 1922 he exhibited a model of an aeroclub that caught the eye of the Vicomte de Noailles, who commissioned him to build a villa on the Côte d'Azur, where this aristocratic rebel could entertain Picasso, Buñuel, Man Ray, and other iconoclasts. Mallet-Stevens went on to design artists' studios, a firehouse, and a row of white cubist houses on a Parisian street that bears his name.

I had the good luck to return to Croix on the eve of the opening. My friend Lauree and I toured the house with Paul-Hervé Parsy, a former Louvre curator who supervised the restoration. In sartorial flair and his insistence on perfection he is a worthy successor to Mallet-Stevens. The ruin had been made whole and proved as much a revelation as the restored Villa Savoie and Eileen Gray's Villa E. 1027. The rigorous minimalism of those modernist landmarks shocked contemporaries; the most surprising thing about the Villa Cavroix is its debt to the *ancien régime*.

The 200-foot-long facade of yellow bricks with its *porte cochère* has the symmetry and grandeur of a traditional château. White marble steps ascend to black lacquered sliding doors that open onto a double-height salon. Curved backlit glass panels with silver trim and chrome wall sconces flank this ceremonial entry and evoke the architect's sets for *L'Inhumaine* and other silent movies. The plan of the villa is formal but, as in the interiors of Adolf Loos, there is no applied ornament, and luxury is expressed in the grain of rare woods and marbles. Away from the rooms where the owners entertained, the mood shifts. One of the boys' bedrooms is a homage to De Stijl: a construction of brightly colored planes. The master bathroom is a temple to hygiene opening onto a terrace. Long balconies overlook an axial pool, which might serve as a landing strip for a seaplane. Hervé insisted that one small room be left unrestored, and the raw brick and crumbling plaster show how great a transformation he wrought. [2015]

Bibliothèque Richelieu: skylit roof vault

BIBLIOTHÈQUE RICHELIEU

On successive trips to Paris, I peered into the two libraries that Henri Labrouste designed in the mid 19th century, but, lacking a reader's card, I was denied entry. When President Mitterand commissioned the Très Grand Bibliothèque as his personal *Grand Projet*, the old national library on the rue Richelieu was closed for restoration and adaptation to a new role. It's now a public showcase and archive, home to manuscripts, photographs, a theater collection, and books on the history of art. The reading room that Labrouste added to the earlier buildings is one of the most glorious, and surprising interiors in the city.

Bibliothèque Richelieu: main reading room

I was shown around by Bruno Gaudin and Virginie Brégal, the architects who are directing the restoration. The long, high-vaulted room is lined with bookshelves and lit from circular openings in shallow domes – an important innovation in an era of gas lighting. The slender cast-iron columns that support this vault anticipate those in Frank Lloyd Wright's Johnson Wax Building, and even Eero Saarinen's Tulip chairs and tables. Over the years, the glass roof above this vault had become so dirty that natural light was blocked; after cleaning, the room has a springtime air, enhanced by the pastoral scenes painted in the lunettes of the arches.

Stone goddesses flank a portal at the far end and beyond is another revelation: multi-level steel bookshelves as austere and functional as any contemporary storage facility, but designed by the same architect, 150 years ago. The contrast is as great as in 19th-century train stations, where a stately facade is grafted onto steel and glass train sheds; Beaux Arts and adventurous engineering back to back. In the foreground is a hydra-headed cluster of steel tubes; a relic of the *pneumatique* that sped messages around the building and even across the city before the era of faxes and email. Gaudin and Brégal have opened up a labyrinth once restricted to staff and scholars, adding bridges and ramps, vitrines and new reading rooms to make the library publicly accessible. [2017]

CERAMIC DELIGHTS

Ceramic panels of children's games at 43 rue Damrémont

A hundred years ago, Montmartre was an artists' colony but it still retained the character of a village. Francisque Poulbot, a local artist best-known for the patriotic posters and postcards he designed during the first World War, inspired a more enduring, though little known art work. Open the door of 43 rue Damrémont in the 18th arrondissement and you are transported back to 1910 when this building was one of many public bath houses built to improve sanitation in poor neighborhoods. The corridor is lined with 12 ceramic panels showing children at play, joyful scenes based on Poulbot's sketches of everyday life in the neighborhood. Here, the kids rule: their parents are hard at work, school is over, and they can splash, and parade, dance in a ring, and hurl snowballs to their heart's content. A medical laboratory occupies the ground floor and the door is open during business hours.

Finding these panels prompted me to revisit the cafés, brasseries, and shops of the Belle Epoque, which delighted in ornament – in carved wood, painted glass, and wrought iron as well as faience. I remembered the witty ceramic murals of the Clown Bar near the Cirque d'Hiver and La Palette on the rue de Seine. And the discovery revived happy memories of La Cigale, a glorious extravaganza in Nantes, and the fishy wonderland of La Huitérie in Lille. Nothing done since has recaptured the verve and assurance of that era. [2017]

LA SEINE MUSICALE

When Renault shuttered its factory on the Île Séguin in the Seine just over the western boundary of Paris, plans for a private art museum were announced and abandoned, and the island is now destined to become a popular cultural resource. Shigeru Ban won the competition to design La Seine Musicale, a complex of spaces that include an expansive plaza, a rock arena, a music school, and a 1,200-seat concert hall enclosed in a flattened glass sphere at the tip of the island: a bubble emerging from a long generic box. The bubble is supported by crisscrossed laminated beams and shaded by a photovoltaic sail that moves with the sun and generates solar power.

Concluding a concert by the Cincinnati Symphony Orchestra at La Seine Musicale

As an architect, Ban is best known for improvisation: a succession of experimental houses in Japan, and temporary structures of cardboard tubes and plastic sheeting to provide shelter after natural disasters around the world. He's used cardboard tubes to support churches and expo pavilions, and they show up in the concert hall, underpinning the red plush seats and casting a lacy veil over the ceiling to diffuse the sound. The walls are clad in undulating milled-wood segments that resemble a giant basket, embracing the audience on different levels and in a gallery that encircles the space.

As Ban showed me around, he mentioned a concert to be held the next day and I was able to scrounge an extra ticket to treat Linda de Nazelle, who adores every kind of music and sings in the choir of Notre Dame. It was the last stop on the European tour of the Cincinnati Symphony Orchestra with their French conductor, Louis Langrée, and it proved a memorable display of virtuosity. The tender romanticism of Dvorzak's Eighth Symphony was bracketed by two sharp-faceted American gems: George Gershwin's *An American in Paris*, and an encore of Leonard Bernstein's *Candide* overture, which the French audience took as a homage to Voltaire. The acoustics were perfect and every instrument stood out clearly. A new edition of the Gershwin made it sound fresh-minted, with subtleties and dissonances that I had never heard before. It was 1928 all over again in a city full of daring innovation. [2017]

Lauree at La Cigale

Dublin: Georgian doorways

IRELAND

Dublin has been the capital of independent Ireland for nearly a century, but the architectural legacy of British rule still defines the city. Georgian squares enclose jungle-like gardens, and arrow-straight streets frame vistas of green hills. Dark brick house fronts are set off by white reveals as crisp as starched collars, and are punched up by vividly painted doors and gleaming brass plates. Behind these harmonious facades lurks a riot of color and ornament. It's a shock to walk through a plain portal and have a nun show you a stair hall that could have strayed north from a palace in Naples. Plaster birds and goddesses cavort on ceilings of searing red and mustard yellow in Belvedere College and 20 Lower Dominick Street. The walls of Ely House seem inspired by a Wedgewood vase, with chaste neo-classical figures on a celadon ground. These exuberant designs were created 200 years ago by Irish craftsmen working alongside Italian stuccoists.

From this time capsule I ventured forth for a week-long drive around Eire, south to Kilkenny, west to Dingle, and north to Galway. It was May and I was blessed by mild sunny weather, and daylight till 11. I stayed in country houses in varying states of decay that welcomed me as though I was an old family friend. One of the joys of a still rural land, living at the pace of 50 years ago, is the warmth of strangers. "It's a grand day," is the universal salutation. Ask directions and you'll get an earful – often to places you hadn't thought of visiting, which suddenly sound to be unmissable. Spend a few minutes admiring a church and someone will bob up to recount its history, back to the Dark Ages.

I remembered an earlier trip when I spent a frustrating hour searching for a house outside Dublin. No mobile phones or GPS in those far-off days, but a local was eager to help. "Jean Duff, you say; I know her well. It's easy. You drive down a way and when you

Stairhall of 20 Lower Dominick Street

come to a turn you pay no attention and keep going past the farm and there's a tree and that doesn't matter at all, and when you come to a sign you have to be careful because the lads turn them around." I nodded. "So, I've been driving in circles because the signs are pointing the wrong way?" "Well, yes and no. Sometimes other boys turn them around again, so they can be pointing the right way some of the time." An hour later, after several wrong turns, I arrived at Jean's doorstep.

Only a few miles separate Galway City from Inishmaan, but this tiny island off Ireland's west coast made me feel as though I was at the end of the earth. "Let us fly you where no one else can," boasts Aer Arann, and its 10-seater plane is the most dependable link to the three Aran Islands. It flies even when winter gales keep the ferry in port. I asked to sit up front with the pilot, a few feet behind the whirling propellers, looking down on the irregular checkerboard of fields enclosed by dry-stone walls, fractured expanses of limestone, and a straggle of hamlets. The plane braked sharply on the short landing strip and taxied over to a waiting Land Rover – one of only four vehicles on the island. I checked into Angela Flaherty's B&B and wandered off along the empty roads.

Stone-Age forts crown two of the hills but, as you approach they merge with later walls, created to clear the ground, subdivide property, and protect the livestock. Lanes link winter and summer pastures and lead down to the coast where seaweed is gathered to fertilize the soil. The stoniness is relieved by the flowering of saxifrage and wild roses, gentian, primroses, and maidenhair fern. A farmer's wife in a red flannel skirt milked her cow beside a new satellite dish. As I climbed, with only birdsong and the sighing of the wind to break the silence, the entire island came into view. The ferry wheeled around to the tiny harbor with its rows of beached curraghs. Beyond was the barren spit of Inisheer, smallest of the islands, and, on the misty horizon, the towering cliffs of Moher.

Only 300 people live on Inishmaan, half what there were before the Great Hunger of 1840. The thatched general store sells postcards of Boston, Mass. – the city to which many islanders emigrated after the famine. Older children go to school on the mainland and many remain there, so the future is uncertain. The pub is a mirror of the contradictions. In the early evening, a row of old men huddle over their pints of ale, murmuring together in Gaelic, while the publican's small son minds the bar and watches television. Soccer and hurling are followed by a segment on yachting in the Caribbean, and *Bay Watch*. Things liven up as a younger crowd arrives. There's traditional music—on fiddle, pipe, and drums—and elaborate dances practiced to perfection on long winter evenings. Around midnight, the party breaks up and people begin to walk home. The sky is still bright, the air is warm, and whitewashed cottages glow like friendly ghosts. [1998]

Inishmaan: arrival

A checkerboard of dry-stone walls

ENGLAND: STRANDED EN ROUTE

I used to write about—and be comped by—luxury hotels. An enjoyable privilege, but sometimes fraught with peril. The publicity director of the London Ritz invited me to lunch the next time I visited the capital. Traveling from LA to Bilbao for the Pritzker Prize dinner in Frank Gehry's Guggenheim, I realized I had a five-hour layover at Heathrow. I dashed to Green Park by tube, had a great meal amid the gilded statuary and potted palms, and left in good time to catch the connecting flight. The train stopped at Baron's Court—a remote westerly suburb—and remained there for ten minutes before the public address crackled, "Due to signals failure, there will be an indefinite delay." A multilingual crowd of frantic fliers besieged the stationmaster. No, he didn't know how long it would take to fix the problem. (A local muttered darkly that it wasn't the signals, but another suicide on the line.) Sorry, but the telephone in his office was for official business, and he couldn't send out a call for taxis.

You'd have better luck hailing a cruising taxi in rural Kansas than in this benighted outpost. Uber hadn't yet arrived. I had only a few pounds in my pocket so I grabbed a couple of French businessmen and began flagging down passing cars. "We'll pay taxi rates if you'll take us to the airport," I said to the first. "Sorry, guv, not going that way," was the response. Another had to hurry home to watch her favorite soap. Time was, if you had waved a crisp five-pound note, a motorist would have driven you to Birmingham. All I had were a few coins.

Finally I sweet-talked a girl who had nothing else to do, and we piled in. I offered her 15 pounds, figuring I could pay a third, when one of the frogs shouted "fifty" like a gambler redoubling his bet. Meanwhile, other refugees from the tube were thumping the window so off we sped. As we reached the terminal, the girl said, "I can't take your money. Why don't you just pay for the petrol?" We kept our promise and the businessmen waved away my share. A quick sprint through a vestigial security check and I caught the flight with seconds to spare. No chance of doing that today. Last time I flew British Airways from Heathrow, my name was scratched when I failed to check in an hour ahead of departure. [1997]

LONDON OPEN HOUSE

Growing up in London, I thought I had exhausted the delights of that sprawling metropolis, from Roman ruins to the newest of the new. Every weekend would find me exploring Wren churches around St. Paul's, searching out an innovative house in some back street, or strolling through a historic estate beside the Thames. What more was left to see? About 500 competing attractions I discovered when I flew back for my first London Open House, an annual event of growing popularity.

The program offered a bewildering choice of cinemas and cemeteries, law courts and livery halls, embassies and entertainment centers. I could take a two-hour tour of the Crossness Sludge-Powered Generator ("Thames Water's state-of-the-art, award-winning building, unique in south-east London"), which would give me bragging rights in any group of seasoned travelers. Regrettably, it was a 45-minute walk from the nearest station. Backstage at the Royal Court Theatre could be interesting, but I'd rather be out front watching the actors. The Old Turkish Baths in Bishopsgate Churchyard had a well-preserved interior, reportedly, but might be a bit compromised by its new role as Ciro's Pizza Pomodoro.

I spread out a map. London is about twenty miles across and aspiring taxi drivers spend years bicycling its streets to acquire "the Knowledge" they'll need to secure a license. A taxi would take me everywhere but the cost for a day would be astronomical. Buses are erratic and subway stations far apart. I called Mary-Ellen Barton, the fearless owner of a red two-seater sports car, and together we plotted an itinerary. Out went the places that had to be pre-booked, or required you to take a guided tour. We didn't want to be lectured to or tied to a schedule. Sludge and pizza were tossed aside. The weekend offered the prospect of a treasure hunt, indulging fantasies and reveling in surprises, so we planned an alternation of the grand and humble, vintage and cutting-edge.

Saturday dawned drizzly; all the better, it would shorten the lines. We arrived early for the star attraction: the Foreign and Commonwealth Office on Whitehall, a trophy of Britain's long-vanished heyday as a world power. The native fondness for queuing in the rain was still alive and well, and a long row of umbrellas extended down King Charles Street. It was a congenial crowd. Everyone we spoke to, in line and later, had attended past events and was eager to share tips and warnings. Heads nodded or shook in disbelief as we produced our list. Strangers argued over alternative choices, additions, and deletions. There was no consensus and I held firm, making a note of places I might see next year. An hour sped by in animated conversation and then we were inside.

There was no band to play Elgar's *Pomp and Circumstance* marches and we didn't see any plumed elephants, but they would have felt entirely at home in these soaring marble halls. In 1858, architect George Gilbert Scott produced a design in the fashionable Gothic style but a new prime minister dismissed this scheme as "the barbarism of the Dark Ages" and demanded it be transformed into a classical palazzo. England was to become the new Rome, and the sculptures of its proconsuls wore togas. Durbar Hall and the Grand Staircase were built to awe Queen Victoria's subjects and allies, but other impressive spaces served the legion of bureaucrats who had long been crammed into a wobbly house on Downing Street with papers stacked in the corridors. Now they are off in functional offices and the empire is gone but these halls are still used for state receptions.

Another whiff of vanished glory lingers in the Art Deco lobby of the *Daily Express* building on Fleet Street. This was the hub of the newspaper world in the 1930s, and Lord Beaverbrook was as eager to impress as Lord Palmerston was with the Foreign Office. The building stood empty for years, gathering dust after the papers decamped to the Docklands in the 1980s, but it has been restored and re-occupied by Goldman Sachs. Poetically apt, for this is the embodiment of bling. Behind the sleek glass and black vitrolite facade is a jazzy confection of gold and silver panels, adorned with star bursts, bas reliefs, and jingoistic slogans. Silver serpent handrails, complete with darting cobra tongues, were recast using old photographs. In *Scoop*, Evelyn Waugh—who was a correspondent for the rival *Daily Mail*—caricatured the pompous Beaverbrook as Lord Copper, and described the lobby as "the Byzantine vestibule of Copper House."

We paused for an early lunch at one of the Fleet Street pubs that once lubricated a pack of journalists and now was deathly still. Still sober, we continued on to Highpoint, an apartment tower on Highgate Hill that's as restrained as the *Express* is flamboyant.

Daily Express lobby

Water pump at the Kew Bridge Steam Museum

They are almost exact contemporaries, but the Russian exile Berthold Lubetkin was an apostle of modernism, with no taste for razzle-dazzle. After designing spiraling ramps for penguins at the London Zoo, he created this rigorous tower for the employees of the Gestetner office equipment company. Le Corbusier waxed enthusiastic, but Lubetkin shocked his purist admirers by substituting Greek caryatids for columns to support the entry canopy of a second, more luxurious tower, reserving the penthouse for himself.

As a Russian who experienced Constructivism first-hand, Lubetkin would have adored the Kew Bridge Steam Museum. Charles Dickens visited this pumping station in 1850 and described the 90-inch Grand Junction engine as "a monster." "You've just time to see the big one," cried the custodian as we arrived, and we raced up a ladder to see the giant piston rising and falling before the retired mechanics who tend these machines switched their attention to another exhibit. All have been withdrawn from active service, but they pump and spin and rotate in turn through the day. The most enthusiastic visitor introduced himself as the fire chief of San Francisco and he climbed down into the steamy cellar to explore the bowels of these great engines.

Our last stop of the day took us from the Industrial Revolution to a medieval barn that is almost as grand as Winchester Abbey, whose canons owned this marvelous structure. It's located in Harmondsworth, close to Heathrow, and the neighboring village may be obliterated if the airport constructs a third runway.

Staircase of the Renaissance St. Pancras Hotel

Sunday's jaunt was no less exotic and varied. We began in Berkeley Square where the last great house of the 1740s, designed by William Kent, has become the Clermont Club, a casino for very high rollers, and Annabel's, a chic basement playpen for gilded youth. The members were surely still asleep as we climbed the double sweep of the staircase, a marvel of baroque exuberance, and admired the portraits of former owners in the gilded salons.

From the priciest club in London to a bingo parlor is a leap, but the Tooting Granada was designed by Thomas Komisarjevsky, a Russian prince, as a movie palace of unrivalled splendor. The painted mirrors, gold encrusted columns, and stained glass must have upstaged all but the most epic movies, but now the only patrons are a few sad old ladies hoping for a modest prize as they check off numbers on their cards.

A similar air of melancholy haunts Nunhead Cemetery in Wandsworth with its tottering tombstones, ruined lodges, and ivy-clad angels. I have a weakness for picturesque decay, and was equally moved by the decrepitude of St. Pancras Chambers. This grand station hotel was then a crumbling ruin with an uncertain future. The Victorians were great engineers, but the steel and glass vaults of the train shed seemed as indecent to them as a naked person, and the prolific Sir George Gilbert Scott concealed it behind a Gothic-style brick palazzo that his namesake, Sir Walter Scott, would have admired. Cobwebs veiled the flaking paint and pigeons flew through the four-story staircase,,but the hotel was recently restored and reopened as the Renaissance St. Pancras, leading out to the steel and glass Eurostar Terminal. [2001]

VICTORIAN SELF-SACRIFICE

One of London's most fascinating sites is centrally located, open every day and rarely visited. Postman's Park, named for its proximity to the Central Post Office, opened in 1880 as a burial ground just north of St. Paul's Cathedral. Twenty years later it incorporated the George Frederic Watts's Memorial to Heroic Self Sacrifice. As the name suggests, it perfectly captures the mix of virtue and pathos in the Victorian era, and the stirrings of social conscience in a deeply polarized society. I never saw it in the years I lived in London, but now it's one of my favorites.

Ceramic plaques, mounted on one wall of the park, commemorate acts of courage by ordinary people, dating from the 1860s through the 1900s. Laborers, their wives and children drown, are consumed in flames, or are crushed by trains in successful and frustrated attempts to save siblings and strangers. Victims include a lady whose carriage topples, a lunatic woman who throws herself on the track, and skaters on thin ice. The heroes were as young as eight and each faced danger unflinchingly. It's deeply moving but faintly melodramatic, for each event evokes a scene from a silent movie. [2007]

Memorial plaques in Postman's Park

STOWE: A WORK TO WONDER AT

An hour's drive northwest of London is Stowe, one of the grandest English country estates. It was created by several generations of the Temple family and a succession of architects. Robert Adam contributed to the design of the great house, which became a prestigious school in 1923 and can be visited during the vacations. There's an oval salon with a coffered vault and Roman frieze, and a music room with Pompeian grotesqueries. The view from the portico supposedly inspired Tom Stoppard's *Arcadia*. William Kent, another architect of genius, improved the landscaping in the 1730s. A contemporary wrote that Kent "leapt over the fence and discovered that all nature is a garden." Scattered around the lakes and meadows are rotundas and temples, arches and columns, a grotto for the resident nymph, and a Palladian bridge. It could be described as a theme park, intended to evoke the classical world and edify the spectator. Ideally, one would come here on a fine day, equipped with a picnic basket, a chilled bottle of Frascati, and a slim volume of Latin pastoral verse, and make a leisurely inspection of the monuments and vistas. Better yet, one can become a temporary resident, by lodging a few nights in the Gothic Temple with its two comfortable bedrooms and rooftop belvedere. If time is short, you can do what I did with a likeminded friend on a hurried visit to my homeland.

We set out from London in the rain, enjoyed a bibulous lunch at Henley, revisited the Chinoiserie rooms at Claydon House, and defied the weather by pressing on to Stowe.

Only two hours remained before closing, so our exploration was far from contemplative, and we borrowed the National Trust buggy to cover more ground. The sky cleared and the sun shone with Roman brilliance, throwing every stone into sharp relief and sparkling off the water. We pretended the roar of speeding cars at the Goodwood track, a few miles away, was distant thunder, and remembered the tribute that Alexander Pope penned when the gardens were new. It was addressed to Lord Burlington, a patron of the arts who returned from the Grand Tour and built Chiswick House. Pope was urging him on when he wrote: "Nature shall join you, time shall make it grow/A work to wonder at – perhaps a Stowe." [2000]

View from the portico of Stowe House

ART ENHANCES NATURE

At the summit of Tejon Pass

The Umbrellas was Christo's most ambitious land art project, a symbolic bridge between California and Japan, which was up for about two weeks. It comprised 1,760 octagonal yellow umbrellas scattered over the sun-scorched hills of the Tejon Pass, 80 miles north of Los Angeles, and 1,340 blue umbrellas amid the paddy fields and farmhouses of Ibaraki Province, 80 miles north of Tokyo. Having missed *Running Fence* (1972) and the wrapped Pont Neuf (1985) I was determined to see both halves of this spectacle.

By good fortune, the umbrellas were raised in California the day I was due to leave on a trip to Japan, so I drove up Interstate 5 in my Mustang convertible and spent a glorious morning in the pass. First one, then a cluster, and finally a line. They seemed alive, like Wordsworth's daffodils, "fluttering and dancing in the breeze." They seemed to have sprouted from barren soil like the flowers that carpet the desert after a wet winter. Many were perched high on ridges where they were backlit or silhouetted against the sky, drawing the eye to the sensuous folds of the hills.

In Japan, a typhoon brought torrential rains, and the umbrellas opened a week late. An American friend and I took the express to Mito, a local train, a bus, a shuttle, and then hired a taxi to drive us around as 900 volunteers completed the installation. In this intimately scaled setting, they appeared surreal, looming over barns, tiled roofs and racks of rice straw, or clustering tightly in a protective embrace. Families stalked these exotic creatures with unabashed delight, and picnicked in their shade as though this were a second cherry blossom festival. [1991]

Christo's Umbrellas, in California and (right) Japan

GATES OF NEW YORK

The Gates in New York's Central Park

It took six years of patient negotiation for Christo and his partner, Jeanne-Claude, to secure the consent of 452 landowners, the Japanese Ministry of Construction, and the River Kuji Fisherman's Union to erect Umbrellas. In New York, 25 years of anguished public debate ended when Mayor Bloomberg authorized the installation of *The Gates* in Central Park. Twenty-three miles of pathway were canopied by fluttering panels of saffron-colored nylon, suspended from 7,500 tall, vinyl frames. Nature-lovers, park commissioners, and affluent neighbors were initially aghast at the prospect of so intrusive a work in their piece of paradise, but the artists overcame all objections, pledging to respect every branch and creating structures that would leave no mark.

Christo was well prepared for this ordeal. Before he fled his native Bulgaria, he was given the task of creating Potemkin villages – prettifying farms along the route of the Orient Express so that affluent Westerners, bound for Paris or Istanbul, would glimpse a seemingly prosperous land, not the squalid reality of a collective state.

I flew to New York for the opening in February 2005, arriving as the last of the banners was unrolled. Over the next three days, in sun and snow, I ranged over the park, from Columbus Circle to Harlem, scrambling up granite outcrops to get a wide view. In their angularity and repetition, the frames played off the sinuous lines of Olmsted's landscape and evoked the tunnel of red torii at the Inari-san shrine in Kyoto. The vibrant banners recalled the fall foliage that the bare trees had shed a few months before. They caught every breeze, fluttering and flying free as an array of flags, and capturing the energy of the city. As the light shifted, they caught the shadows of branches or sparkled in a brilliant ray of sunlight. Joggers glanced up, dogs scampered and barked, and the whole city came to look. Since this was New York, where nearly everyone is outspoken, the volunteers had to answer the predictable questions—"what does it mean?" "How much did it cost?" "Is it art?"—while handing out small samples to discourage souvenir hunters from clipping their own. [2005]

IN PURSUIT OF JUDD

Donald Judd hated the ephemerality and commercialism of New York galleries and bought a disused army base at Marfa, Texas, for the permanent display of his work, alongside other artists he admired. He remodeled the old sheds—which housed German POWs at the end of the war—to serve as galleries. Since his death, the property has been maintained by the Chinati Foundation, long headed by his former companion, the German curator Marianne Stockebrand. I joined Richard Koshalek and a small MOCA group on a visit, driving out through the bleak border country from El Paso.

Marfa still had the character of a frontier town, insubstantial and remote, though a well-stocked bookstore marked the first stage of gentrification. The sheds rattled as long freight trains chugged by. Minimal alterations preserved the rawness, while imposing a sense of order in two rooms of Judd's milled steel boxes, each slightly different from the next, and arranged in a grid pattern. As the wind rose, kicking up billows of dust and clouding the windows, the elemental character of the art became ever more apparent. I spent a solitary hour walking around, mesmerized by the shimmering surfaces and the play of angles. The fluorescent light works of Dan Flavin, the crushed metal sculptures of John Chamberlin, and Kabakov's recreation of an abandoned Soviet schoolroom occupied the neighboring spaces. One had to brave the dust storm to reach these, and that intensified the experience as no museum ever could – though DIA Beacon comes close.

In New York, Judd bought a five-story, cast-iron warehouse at the corner of Spring and Mercer as a live-work space. It cost him $70,000 in 1968; it must be worth a hundred times as much today. ARO did an impeccable restoration, replacing rusted columns and reinstalling hand-made glass in the windows, while leaving the scarred brick walls of the basement in their original condition. It can be visited by appointment on a docent-led tour, and I was pleased to discover that the spirit of Judd still hovered over these empty rooms, as it had when he was a pioneer of the Soho renaissance. Artists camped out in spaces abandoned by industry, before they were sanctioned for living, and long before they and the galleries were priced out by fashionable boutiques.

Judd was a perfectionist and obsessively concerned with precise geometries, but he was also one of the boys, offering jugs of corn whisky to fellow artists on the second floor and hoping they could stumble down one flight of creaky wooden stairs and stay intact. A hand-operated elevator offers an alternative but larger works were craned out of the third-floor studio. There, Judd worked at a stand-up desk, which is still laid out with his measuring tools. The fourth floor has a new Southern pine ceiling and highly polished floor (in contrast to patched industrial floor below) Six of Rietveld's zig-zag chairs are drawn up to the dining table. On the fifth floor, two mattresses are laid out at one end, and at the other there's a sleeping niche for his daughter and a ladder to his son's bunk bed, plus a scatter of art works. It's the perfect expression of *la vie de bohème*: a time capsule of a rougher New York, where creativity flourished in hidden corners of the city. Windows frame handsome neighbors, including a tiny Federal house across Mercer. [2001]

ARTIST DOWN A HOLE

In 2002, I spent ten days in Arizona, researching new architecture for a special issue of the Japanese magazine, *A+U*. James Turrell granted permission to visit Roden Crater, the earth work he was creating in an extinct volcano, on condition I didn't write about it. Two journalists had broken an embargo with stories that emphasized the delays and cost overruns, and made no mention of the artist's vision. I drove to Flagstaff from Phoenix, passing markers for the former settlements of Bloody Basin, Deadman Wash, and Bumble Bee. The despoliation of the West began long ago. A jeep took me over the 156 square miles of ranch land that Turrell acquired to buffer his work from open-cast mining, junk yards, and other eyesores.

At that time, the interventions at Roden Crater had been underway for twenty years, and completion was expected in a year or two. Turrell is a perfectionist and much in demand, for Sky Spaces and other site-specific works. His masterwork is still not finished and may never be. A millennium hence, in the unlikely event that humanity survives that long, archeologists may puzzle over these excavations and speculate on their purpose, as they do at Stonehenge.

A tunnel slopes down from an aperture in the crater. Light from the northernmost setting sun and the southernmost rising moon passes through an iris to focus on a standing stone. An opening will frame the sky above the crater and three down-sloping plinths provide views out over the Painted Desert. I climbed up the unfinished tunnel and trudged through the cinders, recalling my expedition to Haleakala 23 years before. In the clear light I could glimpse the mesas of Monument Valley, 150 miles away. One day, a few lucky aficionados may come here for an experience of nature at its most elemental and retire to the comfortable lodge to await the sunrise. Very few will be there, once every 18.6 years, to glimpse the moon framed in the elliptical opening of the tunnel. [2002]

COOL ARCTIC-TECTURE

In 2003, 17 architects were chosen to collaborate, each with a different artist, on hybrid works of ice and snow in Finnish Lapland. The Snow Show was the brainchild of New York art curator Lance Fung working with the Finnish Tourist Office. I joined a group of journalists on the flight from Helsinki to the small town of Kemi, one of the two locations Fung had selected. A blindingly white expanse of nothingness ended abruptly at a port full of ice-bound ships; we had been crossing the Gulf of Bothnia. In preparation for the trip I had ordered long-johns and snow shoes from L.L. Bean, and retrieved a ski sweater and fireman's coat I had not worn since I left Washington, 25 years before. The cold—45 degrees below—clawed at me as I got off the plane, and I risked frostbite every time I removed a glove to take a photo. The sun hovered on the horizon until four and then vanished until ten the next morning.

A trio of ice maidens

Zaha Hadid's ephemeral ice house in Rovaniemi

By local standards it had been a mild winter, so a few of the structures were being finished as we arrived. The Future Systems/Anish Kapoor dome, resembling a giant strawberry sorbet, had collapsed the previous day due to faulty wiring that overheated the interior. The others, built by volunteers with advice from an engineer, held up well and showed how much could be achieved with two basic materials. A team from Athens created an amphitheater, substituting ice for stone. Rachel Whiteread modeled the interior of an East London house, and Tadao Ando created a tunnel that glowed with the neon numbers of Tatsuo Miyajima, gleaming like tiny points of fire. We went to an ice hotel for dinner and returned to see how lighting transformed the translucent slabs. Afterwards, I joined Alan Riding, cultural correspondent for the *New York Times* and, after warming ourselves with plentiful shots of vodka, we went carol singing, serenading the locals with "a poor man gathering fuel"and other familiar ditties.

Next day a bus took us to Rovaniemi, a town that was replanned by Alvar Aalto following its destruction by the retreating Nazi forces. That seemed an appropriate setting for a short-lived exhibition and the ephemeral character of the work on show was dramatically reinforced on the second night. Cai Guo-Qiang set fire to Zaha Hadid's ziggurat, turning it into a baked Alaska as flaming vodka coursed from the upper terraces, prompting the fire brigade to join the excited spectators. And then nature took over, producing a stunning display of the Northern Lights. The sky rippled from horizon to horizon with pale green light and the structures acquired an unearthly presence far transcending anything the architects and artists could have imagined. [2004]

DESIGN HOTELS

I have a weakness for design hotels, even though they are often too clever for their own good, putting form ahead of function, and substituting attitude for service. One of the best is the Puerta America in Madrid, a 12-story block by Jean Nouvel, with guest rooms and public spaces by 15 other architects and designers. It's a layer-cake of surprises. The facade is garish, with two rainbow-hued wings highlighted in neon, a cluster of five glass elevators, and a giant orange canopy. Step inside John Pawson's minimalist lobby and you wonder if it's the same building. Zaha Hadid designed the first floor of guest rooms and the hotel smartly charges a premium to stay there. Each is a seamless capsule of white Corian, which swells and folds to provide shelves, benches, storage, and a platform bed. A white Corian armchair sits on a white carpet and when the sun flooded in I had to put on my shades. There's a choice of all-white and all-black bathrooms and the huge tubs must be a popular rendezvous for weekend escapades.

It was hard to tear myself away from Hadid, but in the interest of research I sampled Norman Foster (cool and precise), Marc Newson (sleek expanses of gray acrylic opening off a blood-red corridor), Arata Isozaki (a shadowy zen retreat), Javier Mariscal ('50s kitsch) and a few that should have remained on the drawing board.

It reminded me of other unconventional hostelries I've stayed in: a succession of Philippe Starck hotels for Ian Schrager, particularly the Delano in South Miami Beach; Andrée Putnam's transformation of a water tower in Cologne; and, most memorable, the Hotel Il Palazzo in the red light district of Fukuoka, Japan. Aldo Rossi designed it as a windowless temple, and invited Ettore Sottsass and Shiro Kuromata to design bars as dysfunctional art works. The staff wandered around in a daze, avoiding eye contact with the few guests; nothing better exemplified the short-lived excess of Japan in the 1980s.

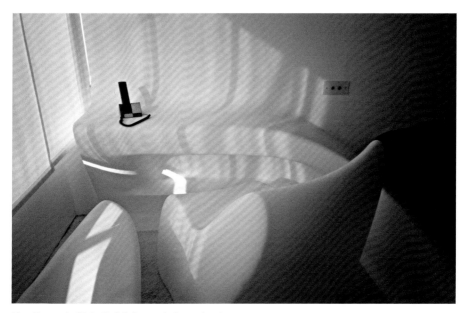

The white womb of Zaha Hadid's decor at the Puerta America

Roof terrace of the Unité in Marseilles

Far more rewarding are the guest rooms in Le Corbusier's Unité d'Habitation in Marseilles. They are almost as frugal as those in the monastery of La Tourette, though they do have private showers. A few years ago they were refurbished, and a fine restaurant was added at the other end of the third floor. The architect designed it as a shopping street for residents, but the stores failed for lack of custom. Now vendors' vans bring meat and fish to the front door. In contrast, the roof terrace is intensively used: by small children in the elevated day care center; by aerobics classes; and a dozen other impromptu activities. I was content to sit on one of the concrete benches and admire what Corbu called "the masterly, correct, and magnificent play of masses brought together in light" while sipping a pastis. [2005/2015]

SPAIN: SEVILLE FERIA

The Feria of Seville began as a horse fair, and it's held in an open space across from Luisa Park. In his 1950 book, *Spain*, the English writer Sacheverell Sitwell gave a wonderful description of the spectacle – though it helped that he was a guest of the Duke of Alba and was driven around in a liveried carriage. Even without those advantages, you can have a great time – as I did when I first went there . As long as the Spanish love to see and be seen and breed elegant horses, the Feria will keep its magic. Those two ingredients are combined in the morning *paseo*, when traditionally attired couples ride slowly back and forth on the dusty avenue, the man sitting boldly upright, his wife or fiancée side-saddle behind him with her brilliantly colored flounced dress spread over the horse's rump, her black hair drawn tightly back, and a rose behind her ear. Children follow suit; horsemanship must be in their genes.

In the early evening, after a leisurely lunch and long siesta, the entertainment begins. Private and public *casetas*—open-fronted canvas enclosures—are set up around the perimeter to provide food and wine, music and flamenco. Some don't get underway until the early hours of the morning and it's worth making a detour to the Barrio Santa Cruz, a labyrinth of white walls and narrow lanes that was once the Jewish quarter, but most resembles a North African casbah. There, in the moonlight, Sitwell "heard the sound of voices, and in the tiled space around a fountain found a group of young men and two young women; one unslung his guitar, the others clapped hands rhythmically, there was a crackle of castanets, and the younger of the two girls began to dance the *seguidilla*." That was written nearly 70 years ago, but Feria and other Spanish fiestas can still deliver enchanting surprises. [1962]

Seville: Barrio Santa Cruz

Children riding in the Feria

SURREAL RETREAT

Emilio Ambasz is an architect whose work often verges on fantasy, nowhere more so than the Casa de Retiro Espiritual, 30 km north of Seville. Part folly, part retreat, it first appears as a white cube on a hilltop, with a door at one corner and wooden mirador above. Nothing could be more typical of Andalusia but, when you walk around, the cube reveals itself to be an illusion: two blank walls set at 90 degrees to each other with a precipitous steel staircase set diagonally on each inner face, converging at the mirador. I climbed, clinging tightly to the recessed handrail and dared myself to look down from the mirador at the tiny figure of the custodian, and out over rolling country to a lake.

Emilio Ambasz's Casa de Retiro Espiritual

The real house is underground, lit from a sunken courtyard and from skylights set into a grassy bank. An L-plan salon opens through glass sliders onto a white columned portico. Contrasting with this ethereal white space are brilliant yellow bathrooms, and a meditation room with gold niches set into Prussian blue walls. Ambasz had designed red leather armchairs and glass tables but, as yet, no bed. Even so, it was a covetable hideaway. [2005]

Seville Parasol in the Plaza de la Encarnación

URBAN PARASOL

On a recent visit to Seville, I went to see Jürgen Mayer's Metropol Parasol. Civic icon, shady plaza, farmers' market, archeological museum, and belvedere: the city's latest landmark plays many roles. It resembles a grove of prefabricated wooden trees soaring over the drab Plaza de la Encarnación, which was excavated for an underground parking garage. Digging was halted when mosaic floors and fragments of Roman villas were found at a depth of six meters. Three competitions were held to redevelop the site and Mayer won the last.

Most innovative urban interventions—from the Eiffel Tower to Disney Hall—provoke hostility and take years to win public acceptance. To their credit, Sevillanas saw that Mayer had been inspired by the trees in a neighboring park and the undulating roof of their Gothic cathedral. They may also have noticed allusions to the fretted screens and patterned bricks of Mudejar buildings, and the barred shadows of the awnings covering the Calle Sierpes in summer.

To preserve the integrity of the ruins, Mayer supported the structure at a few points, enclosed the Roman remains, laid out a new paved plaza beneath a canopy that rises from six trunks, and created a new home for the market. Steps and escalator in concrete shafts ascend to a rooftop restaurant and an 800-foot walkway that snakes over an undulating grid of laminated wood panels. Other Mayer buildings can appear mechanistic; the Parasol has the organic quality of a honeycomb or a coral reef, transcending the limitations of simple modules to create an urban landscape. [2011]

SAETAS IN OSUNA

Tour buses throng Seville, Cordoba and Granada, swamping the celebrated sites, but Andalusia is full of historic towns they pass by. I spent a wonderful day in Osuna, with its palaces and churches, Renaissance and rococo facades, and pebbled Plaza Mayor. A grumpy nun showed me the pretty tiled cloister of the Encarnacion Church, objecting to the fact I was alone. Jesus Christ would have had a hard time here unless he had brought a busload of apostles. However, while we were disputing my singularity I heard an unearthly wail drifting from the church and went inside. I had chanced on the finals of a saeta competition. Saeta is Spanish for arrow and for traditional songs of lamentation, and both terms applied to what I was hearing.

The church was full of locals come to cheer their favorites, and the contestants were sober-suited men who stepped forward in turn to emit a cry that was harsh yet melodious. The tonalities were Arab, a legacy of the 700-year Moorish occupation and a reminder that parts of north Africa are on the same latitude as the south of Spain. One after another, they sought to stretch a few breaths into an aria of pain and joy that resounded from the lofty vault and would be heard again during the penitents' parades of the Semana Santa. Though an atheist, I find such sounds deeply moving and oddly reminiscent of boys' choirs in English cathedrals, hitting the high notes of motets by Tallis and Byrd. [1992]

PORTUGAL

It's easy to drive though Portugal in ten days and see it as a much-diminished variant of Spain. Look close and its distinctive features become apparent. Every time I go there, I make new discoveries and delight in the unique character of the architecture, past and present.

Main Street and square of Monsarz

Azulejos in the Palacio de la Fronteira, Lisbon

Lisbon: Rossio Square

Jerónimos monastery cloister in Belem

I would start in Monsarz, a one-street village in the mountains that divide the two countries. The trim black and white facades, impeccably maintained, are quite different from those across the border. Evora was a Roman foundation that flourished in the Renaissance and then declined. There are no great monuments. But stay in the pousada and stroll the cobbled streets, admiring the tailored stone curbs and the way a tiny square becomes a showpiece of urbanity. Standouts include the white marble fountain in the Largo da Puerta do Mouro, and the chapel of bones in the church of San Francisco.

Fountain in Largo da Puerta do Mouro, Evora

The beauty of Lisbon on its estuary and the new town created by the Marquis de Pombal after the earthquake of 1755 needs no further celebration, but be sure to see the Palacio de la Fronteira and its terraced garden, lined with marvelous azujelos. Other highlights include the black and white pavements, the Jeronimos Monastery, where stone acquires a tropical exuberance, and a scatter of bizarre statues. The new MATA museum of architecture is a lively addition to the waterfront.

Opporto is still the center of the port wine trade, but it's also home base for the country's leading architects, Alvaro Siza and Eduardo Souto de Mouro. Priorities include Siza's Serralves Art Foundation (even though it often presents mediocre art), his Marques de Canavares church, and dinner at his first project, the Boa Nova Tea House. Rem Koolhaas's Casa do Musica hosts a diversity of concerts, and the posada at Amares, which Souto de Moura created within an old monastery, is a good base for exploring the region.

That includes Monsanto, where houses grow out of massive boulders, and the espigueiros of Lindoso. An espiguero is a stone container for the storage of grain, raised on stumpy pillars with wide capitals to prevent rats from climbing inside. You find them throughout northern Portugal and Spain, but the finest collection is clustered on a hillside in Lindoso beside the threshing field. Each has its individuality and some have acquired the patina of age or a coat of lichen. They resemble raised

Espigueiros in Lindoso

tombs and, legend has it, they go walking at night. It's a melancholy spectacle, quite apt for the land of fado.

Lisbon: Gulbenkian and friend; statue in Praca Quintelana

Portugal has been transformed over the past 50 years, but it still retains its character as the quirky western edge of Europe. It's an odd mix of old and new. Poverty preserved its historic legacy from the age of the explorers, when the country was enriched by its colonies. After a long decline it emerged from isolation and joined the European Union. That brought a measure of prosperity, and every old town is now encircled by an ugly band of spec-built houses. On the plus side, the native zeal for homicidal driving has been tamed by the new motorways and it's much easier to get around. [1992/2016]

GERMANY: BERLIN

Berlin was divided when I first went there in the 1970s, and the Wall was the defining feature of the city. Conspicuous consumption, neon, and sleek Mercedes on one side; ruins and a pervasive grayness on the other, with the occasional Trabant hiccuping its way in a cloud of exhaust down empty avenues. One Sunday there was a military parade on the Unter der Linden. Gray-uniformed soldiers goose-stepped behind the same Roman-style standards that I remembered from *Triumph of the Will*. The regime that proclaimed hostility to fascism had embraced its props and, in Stasi, its methods. The Wall was a counter-culture canvas to the West, with platforms from which one could peer over; to the east it was isolated by barbed wire and minefields, and the guards had orders to shoot anyone who ventured across. Checkpoint Charlie, now a tourist trap, was a potential flashpoint that might easily have sparked an exchange of fire.

Flash forward, and that death-zone has been built over; only a fragment of the wall remains, beside a memorial park that traces the routes of escape tunnels. The Mitte is once again the beating heart of the city and working class districts have been gentrified. East and West have become one. Foster's transparent dome atop the Reichstag and Libeskind's Jewish Museum symbolize the renaissance, as do the restored Museum Island and the reconstructed Royal Palace.

Those draw the crowds, but every time I return, I'm reminded how much survives from the 1920s, when Berlin was a crucible of modernism in architecture, science, and the arts. The AEG Turbine Factory is still performing as well as it did in 1909. Within Peter Behrens' stylized temple of stone and riveted steel beams, overhead cranes carry the vast steel assemblies, and craftsmen finish each by hand with same care that would go into the engine of a racing car. Cubist villas in the West End have been restored; Mies's Lemke House in the east is now a small museum. Six Berlin housing complexes of the 1920s have been named a UNESCO World Heritage Site. There are a hundred more buildings to delight the aficionado. Extraordinary that so many key works survived the devastation of war, and I wanted to immerse myself in that world.

The U-Bahn that whisked me from Mitte to the Horseshoe housing estate doubles as a time machine. In 25 minutes I was transported back to the Weimar era, when this land-scaped community of modest dwellings was built on a manorial property at the edge of the

East Berlin under communism: the ruined cathedral; Goose-stepping guard

Abandoned car on the western side of the Wall; Trabant as an art object

city. Low-rise blocks radiate out from the horseshoe of apartments that gives the project its name. The Hufeisensiedlung still looks as it did in the 1920s – only the cars are new. The landscaping has been restored along with the vibrant colors on the facades.

A pedestrian path leads from the Parchimerallee station to a modest white house, set back behind apple trees and climbing roses. I stepped inside and found myself in a world of color, created by architect Bruno Taut, and impeccably restored by graphic designer Ben Buschfeld and his wife, landscape architect Katrin Lesser. "We thought we would create a museum but we couldn't secure funding and decided to rent it to visitors who share our passion for modernism," says Buschfeld. "Architecture and design are meant to be used and the only way to experience a house is to live in it."

Photomural of Berlin in 1945 in front of the restored Brandenburg Gate

Horseshoe housing estate (left) and the Taut House living room (right)

"We didn't intend to buy a second house," admits Buschfeld, "but we accompanied some friends to one that an old lady had recently vacated. They were shocked by its bad condition, but we were thrilled to find so much of the original fabric was intact." Their offer was accepted and they embarked on a program of restoration that would extend over two years. Taut's colors had been painted over many times, so the couple sought advice from Berlin architect Winfried Brenne, who had restored the polychrome facades of the estate in the 1990s. He recommended two experts, who compiled an 80-page report on the varied colors of each surface, scraping away to reveal the original layer.

At the end of the first year, the house was repainted. The front door and window frames were highlighted in blue. Floors are red in each room and gray in the circulation areas; walls range from a soft green living room to vibrant blue and yellow bedrooms. Stair banisters alternate between red and white with a black handrail, and the stoves add a rich glow. Then the couple went searching for period furnishings at antique shows, flea markets, and on eBay.

The Tautes Heim, as the couple call their trophy, captures a moment in time when society seemed to be entering a new and more hopeful age; a world made new. The colors are joyful and exuberant, lighting up the long gray days of winter and adding a feeling of warmth on chilly evenings. The Hufeisensiedlung was a paradise for early residents, many of whom moved from oppressive, overcrowded tenements, and there's still a waiting list to buy property here.

In 1932, Count Harry Kessler brought André Gide to see the new estates, and recorded the French writer's appreciation in his diary. "Why should the French have entirely lost their feeling for architecture, whereas in Germany it has suddenly blossomed forth?" asked Gide, and Kessler responded: "To look on this architecture simply as architecture, art for art's sake so to speak, is to miss its point. It has to be understood as a new way of living, a new assessment of what life is for and how it should be lived." [1970/2016]

* * *

Back in the city I went to see the Feurle Collection, where Daniel Maruca, the director, showed me around. A reinforced concrete-block house designed for use as a wartime communications center, then used for storage, was adapted by John Pawson to be a private museum for a German collector of Asian art. The basement, flooded by the Landwehr canal, had to be drained and dried out. Within the massive shell, 12 feet thick, a grid of columns supports the 2,000 square meter spaces on ground and basement levels, plus a water court that extends out from the basement and is viewed through glass.

I entered through a dark room, listening to three minutes of John Cage, then into a hall in which the only illumination is from tightly focused pin spots that highlight small Khmer stone sculptures and cast their shadows across the floor. It's as though one were exploring Angor Wat by moonlight. Raw concrete, black steel balustrades and plinths, and raw Thai silk drapes are juxtaposed as a foil to precisely positioned objects below, and Chinese lacquer furniture on the ground floor. It's a triumph of minimalism, architecture in the service of art. [2016]

DRESDEN

An express train from Berlin took me to Dresden early on a fine Sunday morning and as I strolled along the Brühl terrace overlooking the Elbe, I marveled at how it had changed since my first visit. The sun glinted off newly gilded spires and domes, and church bells rang out over a city that has regained its former glory. The historic center, devastated in the bombing raid of February 1945, looks much as it did in the views that Bernardo Bellotto painted, 250 years ago. Frauenkirche, the protestant cathedral, has been rebuilt from a vast pile of rubble. The exterior is a jigsaw puzzle of new and fire-scorched stones but the interior is pure theater with curved pews, a tier of balconies, and walls painted in ice-cream colors to resemble street facades.

The greatest monument of Dresden is the Zwinger, a baroque pleasure palace with a vast courtyard intended for festivities and tournaments. The stone figures that line the courtyard—some cleaned, some still blackened—supporting bays and crowning parapets, are like petrified guests at a grand reception. Crowns, eagles, and coats of arms symbolize the power of the Elector of Saxony, and Augustus the Strong appears as Hercules supporting the globe. Raphael's *Sistine Madonna*, Giorgione's *Sleeping Venus*, as well as canvases by Botticelli, Titian, and Vermeer are showcased alongside extraordinary collections of armor and porcelain. Across the street is the royal palace, which contains the Green Vault, one of a complex of museums. A succession of lavishly decorated rooms display secular and sacred objects in gold, silver, and ivory; rich jewels and such curiosities as miniature stags with coral antlers, and Nautilus shells transformed into chariots, boats, and animals.

A different kind of exotica can be found in the Pfund Dairy of 1892. Walls and ceilings are covered in richly patterned and modeled Villeroy & Bosch tiles: a mix of Renaissance cartouches, cherubs operating milk machines, and gold medals won in long-ago trade fairs. The former Yenidze cigarette factory was named for a town in Turkey and is closely modeled on an Ottoman mosque. This colorful extravaganza sparkles anew and is now owned by the municipality, which organizes readings for children beneath the stained glass dome, and leases the seventh floor to a restaurant that offers panoramic views over the city.

Dresden is a city of museums, but it has resisted the urge to turn itself into one, and has embraced the best of every era, including the present. The main synagogue, which was completed in 2002 replacing one the Nazis torched and later demolished, is outwardly plain: a tilted block clad in stone shingles. Within is a draped canopy of golden rings, evoking Moses's tent, set off by fine joinery. The UFA-Palast, a 12-theater multiplex designed by the Viennese firm of Coop Himmelblau is located on a commercial street that was stodgily rebuilt in the 1970s; it soars like a soufflé in a row of dumplings. Stairs and open walkways dance through the luminous void of the lobby, and there is a tiny circular coffee bar suspended within a cone of cables. Most daring is Daniel Libeskind's addition to the Military History Museum: a concrete and steel wedge that crashes into a neo-Renaissance barracks in a reference to the bombs that rained down on the city.

For music and opera, the Semper is one of Germany's greatest theaters. One evening I went to collect a reserved ticket for The *Magic Flute*. A stern-faced woman began shaking her head before my escort had finished talking. No, she hadn't received a request from the press office; no, there were no tickets left. It seemed like a rerun of the years when all the

Dresden reborn: the Frauenkirche

The Zwinger palace at the heart of Dresden

seats were reserved for apparatchiks. A renewed attack breached the wall. An usher took me to the rear and set up a chair in the aisle. The production was an enchantment and, at intermission I emerged onto the Theaterplatz, to replay the arias in my head, and revel in the décor of floodlit buildings.

To appreciate the beauty of the city in its heyday, you should head east to the Panometer, a *trompe l'oeil* panorama of Dresden as it appeared in 1756, housed in a rotunda that was formerly a gas storage tank. Painted canvases created by hand and computer simulation, meticulously researched from old maps and prints, line the interior. They show a city still bounded by its walls, hugging the river, with one bridge and the countryside close at hand. Fashionable strollers gather in the now-vanished Bulow gardens, and a cross-section of the population throng the streets. The panorama can be viewed from three levels, each providing a different perspective and exerting a compelling power – especially when the lights dim to evoke nightfall.

Another time capsule is a two-hour drive or train ride to the east. Goerlitz is a tiny gem that straddles what is now the German-Polish border. Miraculously, it survived the war unscathed. A succession of painted baroque facades rise from the two market places and quiet cobbled streets. There are no grand monuments, just a pervasive delight in color, texture and detail that is an authentic part of everyday life. [2008]

BAVARIA

Nowhere was rococo embraced with such ardor as in Bavaria. For most tourists it's the land of beer gardens and the fanciful castles of Ludwig II, which anticipate those of Disney. For me it's Wieskirche, an enchanting village church, and the restored treasures of Munich. To wander through the golden salons of the Residenz and attend a chamber opera in the Cuivilliés Theater is the height of pleasure. Above all it's the Amalienburg, a hunting pavilion in the park of Nymphenburg, created in the 1730s by the court architect, François de Cuivilliés. There are kennels for the dogs, a kitchen with Delft tiles, and small painted rooms. Everything pales beside the central salon. The *Spiegelsaal* is the perfect setting for a costume ball or a program of Mozart quartets. Johann Baptist Zimmerman created the stuccoes, silver on pale blue walls, receding to infinity in the mirrors. The effect is as delicate as a cloud of foam rising from the undulating wave of the cornice. Nereids and cherubs are tangled in nets, birds scud across the sky, musical instruments alternate with trophies of the chase. Blown-glass chandeliers add sparkle, but my favorite time is winter, when sunlight is reflected off snow, making the room even more ethereal. [1987/2005]

Stuccoes in the Spiegelsaal of the Amalienburg

ROUTE OF INDUSTRY

For much of the 20th century, Germany was the leading industrial power in Europe, and the mines and steelworks of the Ruhr enriched the Krupps and fuelled two world wars. The relics attract a stream of pilgrims to what has become the Route of Industry.

The Zeche Zollverein is a coal washing plant near Essen, commissioned in 1932 by a client who belonged to the Werkbund and wanted to take a fresh approach to industry. It was spared from bombing during war because the credits to British and American banks

The Zeche Zollverein; functional architecture repurposed

had not been repaid. Austere dark brick buildings with orange steel bands are laid out with the same regularity as Mies van der Rohe's campus for the Illinois Institute of Technology. The main lift serves as an entry portal to the complex. Two blocks flank an allée leading to the administrative tower; tricks of Renaissance perspective make it seem longer. Foster & Partners turned the boiler house into a design museum; OMA created an orange staircase; a school is off to one side. Other blocks house the Ruhr Museum of local history or are leased to designers and artisans.

Volklinge Hutte is a decommissioned steel works outside Saarbrucken. Here is the underground city of *Metropolis* in ruins, the Moloch furnaces cold, the workers gone; grass and trees replacing the toxic gases; a moving

Volklinge Hutte, a rusted monument of heavy industry

spectacle – for its vast scale and as a monument to the transitoriness of human affairs. No lions or lizards in these ruins; just the soaring towers of rusted steel, the conveyor belts and pulleys. The core is surprisingly compact. A raised walkway provides a good overview of the tangle of wheels and trusses at the base; an elevator ascends to the top loading gallery, 100 feet up, from which you can walk among the furnace lids and view the exhaust vents close-up.

Far to the south, in Friedrichshafen on the shore of Lake Constance, the Zeppelin Museum is housed in a train station close to where the airships were made and it does a good job of capturing the scale and wonder of this engineering triumph. There's a mockup of one section of the light metal cage and of the gondola for the 100 passengers and crew, with tiny cabins and expansive lounges and dining rooms. The Nazis used it for propaganda purposes and the crash of the Hindenburg was given only a passing mention in the party newspaper. There's a piece of the wreckage, which carries the same symbolic freight as fragments of the World Trade Center in New York. The museum restaurant evokes the passenger dining room with similar lightweight tubular metal furniture. [2008]

Hamburg from the Elbe

The Free and Hanseatic City of Hamburg boasts two UNESCO World Heritage sites. Speicherstadt is an island complex of bonded warehouses astride a canal, which are now being converted into apartments and studios. Fritz Hogär's Chilehaus is a masterpiece of 1920s Expressionist brick-work, with a sharp prow that evokes the clipper ships of an earlier time. Its shape is echoed in the Elbphilharmonie, a *Stadtkrone* that dominates the skyline as a cathedral does in older cities. It has become the new icon of Hamburg: a frozen wave of glass that seems to fly over the water, like the sails of the Sydney Opera House.

Chilehaus evokes the bow of a clipper

Herzog & de Meuron's concept was acclaimed from the start—by the public and planners—and retained its integrity through 13 years of design development and stop-go construction. The architects sketched a glass-clad complex extruded from a vintage warehouse, treating it as a plinth. Apartments and a hotel would wrap around two centrally located auditoriums; parking, support spaces, public amenities and mechanical services would be accommodated in the warehouse.

The new structure, rising to a peak of 29 stories, is clad in a double layer of warped glass panels printed with 500 different dot patterns to provide thermal insulation, frame views, enrich the facades, and provide a point of reference for ships' radar. Surface patterns have long been a signature feature of this firm, and here they've created a sparkling crystal,

The Elbphilharmonie is Hamburg's new civic icon. Above, from the Elbe; below, the main auditorium

which changes shape as you move around it, and goes from dark to reflective as shifts of light illuminate its facets. The bottom floor, containing a public plaza is recessed and opens onto terraces with arches that frame views of city and harbor to east and west. The roof is a fifth facade of eight concave surfaces.

A curved escalator slices through the warehouse, launching concertgoers and visitors on an architectural promenade that continues to the upper levels of the main auditorium. Brick gives way to oak, exposed concrete to Venetian plaster, and strip to rounded ceiling lights as one ascends stairs whose angular complexity evokes the drawings of M.C. Escher. A glass-capped lightwell provides vistas up and down. All this builds anticipation for the main event: a four-level concert hall of dazzling virtuosity. The vineyard plan of Scharoun's Berlin Philharmonie was a point of departure but the architects looked to earlier models to create a new typology. "We were inspired by the Greek theater, which is carved from stone, to give gravity to a concert hall that is up in the air," says Herzog. "Another important ingredient is the soccer stadium with its steep tiers to create a strong interaction between audience and players. And third is the tent-like roof that you find in the Bayreuth Festspielhaus – the notion of a suspended fabric canopy, rather than a dome or acoustic panels."

The auditorium can best be appreciated from the top level, where its verticality is most evident, and the blocks of seating are spaced out by the richly textured walls and sculptured oak balustrades. Blocky gray seats are designed to absorb sound in the unlikely event that any remains unoccupied. Three internal circulation routes spiral down from the stacked lobbies, linking seating areas and bringing concertgoers together. The three-level organ pipes shimmer in a soft light and enrich this visual expression of the excitement of classical music at its best. Sight and sound are fused to achieve the sublime. [2016]

LURE OF TRAVEL

Every year I agonize over where in the world I shall go. Architecture is my passion, and I'm a city mouse who feels out of place in the countryside. Trees and mountains are fine as backdrops, but it's streets, squares, and intricate facades that excite me. I usually travel alone, with no one to please but myself. I love surprises and hate crowds, but find myself constantly tugged back to the places I'm most familiar with: to London where I grew up; to Paris, where I've always wanted to live; to New York, Tokyo, and Berlin. I know my way around those sprawling metropolises; there are friends to catch up with, old haunts to revisit, and new attractions to explore. The list of things to do and see, from a major monument to a deft conversion, a can't miss exhibition to a minor museum in the outer suburbs – is inexhaustible, but a tad exhausting. For a change of pace, as some might go to a spa or a beach to decompress, I take off to a compact city that I can walk around and get to know in a week.

I'm looking for islands on the land that haven't been submerged by the tide of mass tourism; places that have a unique flavor, with residents who welcome strangers because they don't see too many of them. Most are on the fringes of Europe, in countries that were long isolated by politics or geography and had to be feisty to survive. In some, the spirit of resistance to a powerful neighbor is reflected in the architecture, or in a language that's unintelligible to everyone else. For me it's a delight to be the only foreigner in a restaurant, chatting with a waiter who speaks a familiar tongue and can guide me through a linguistic labyrinth to flavors and aromas I'll long remember. Here, and around the city, I feel free as a child wandering off by myself, knowing that I will always find someone to translate or give directions in English or French, or a hybrid I can puzzle out. [2002]

LJUBLJANA

Ljubljana: Cuden House, Dragon Bridge

Getting to Slovenia, a republic that declared independence in 1991, and was spared the bloodbath that engulfed other provinces of the former Yugoslavia, was harder than I expected. I thought of driving from Austria but there was a mile-long line of vehicles waiting to cross the border. It was only an hour on the autostrada from Venice, but in 2002 Italian rental agencies wouldn't allow me to take a car across the border. The Slovenians were happy to help, promising to meet me at the Friuli-Trieste airport so I could drive across in one of their automobiles.

My target was Ljubljana, the pocket capital. During the four decades of socialism there were some klutzy additions, but the center still looks much as it did in 1900. An earthquake had devastated the city and the Austrian rulers rebuilt it in Jugendstijl and neo-Renaissance style. That provides a sympathetic context for the work of Jože Plečnik, who spent his long life (1872–1957) enriching the capital with monuments, obelisks, and landscaping, as well as churches, offices, a football stadium, and a cemetery. His masterpiece is the University Library, a large brick block with inset stones that catch the light. A grandiose gray marble staircase flanked by urns and columns leads to the functionalist reading room. He designed a trio of bridges over the river to a cobbled circle and it is there that the urbane diversity of Ljubljana snaps into focus. The clock tower of the castle sails high above the wooded hillside, the loggia of Plečnik's market defines the further bank, and the baroque Franciscan church anchors the circle.

At the castle I asked an attendant if I could park there – since most of the places were reserved for a wedding. "Where are you from?" "Los Angeles," I answered. He waved his arms excitedly. "Have you seen John Wayne?" he asked. "Not lately; he passed away," I replied. "And Kirk Douglas and William Holden? They are alive?" Hollywood loves guys like this. The agency representative was waiting for me at the airport. I asked what the excess hours on the rental would cost. He smiled and shrugged, "No charge; we want you to be happy and come back." [2002]

BUDAPEST

Though the Budapest rising of 1956 was brutally suppressed, Hungary asserted its independence from Soviet dogma long before the Wall came down. The capital sparkles anew and you can see how it aspired to outshine Vienna when it was made the second capital of the Austro-Hungarian Empire in the late 19th century. Socialist monuments have been relocated to Statue Park, a graveyard of failed dreams on the outskirts of the city. There you will find petrified tableaux of muscular workers striding forward to an earthly paradise, comrades exchanging manly handshakes, party officials in boxy suits, and kerchiefed women with good childbearing bodies. Lenin declaims from a rostrum but Stalin is reduced to his boots – all that was left when his statue was torn down. It's a sad mix of delusion and oppression; a parade of kitsch with a sinister sub-text. There's added poignancy now that the country is retreating into chauvinistic nationalism. [2007]

A revolutionary deported to Statue Park

ROMANIA

On the map, it looked like a leisurely scenic drive from Sighisoara, birthplace of Vlad the Impaler, to the painted monasteries of Bucovina. As I soon learned, it's foolish to count on anything but surprises in Romania. A detour through the gypsy quarter of Reghini—mustachioed men striding along in dark suits and broad brimmed hats, women scurrying after in long multicolored skirts and jingling bangles—led me onto a different road than the one I had planned to take. But this was national highway 17, and sure to be just as fast.

I guessed wrong. The potholes began at once; the construction sites soon followed. Every few miles, the convoy of trucks and a few beleaguered motorists were stopped to allow oncoming traffic to negotiate the mud patch beside the road gang hacking away with picks and shovels. A stretch of new pavement gave hope that one had reached the end of this obstacle course, but in no time, CRASH, the car thudded over the edge of the asphalt and back into the potholes, rocking from side to side as the rain streamed down. Five hours and seventy miles later, I reached Gura Humor.

I hadn't come this far, driving alone in search of authenticity, to stay in the looming Best Western at the center of town. A hand-lettered sign pointed me towards Casa Christian, a B&B that a Romanian friend had booked me into. My host, Constantin, was tending his roses and bounded out to greet me, his arms flung wide. "You have come!" he exclaimed. "Thank you very much!" Effusively, he led me to the second floor of the tin-roofed, wood-paneled house that he—a retired engineer—had built for his family. An expansive suite of rooms opened onto a verandah overlooking the town and the roses. Dinner was prepared by his wife and his mother and I was served in solitary state. It was the best meal of the trip by far: garden vegetables in a cold ratatouille, aromatic soup, roast chicken from

Rural vernacular: carved wooden gate

a neighbor's farm, freshly baked spice cake, effervescent white wine bought from the priest, and, finally, a searing shot of home-made prune palintsa.

Basking in Constantin's hospitality and applauding his children's virtuosity on the piano and violin, I wondered at the absence of other guests. His face darkened. "So this beeg shot from Bucharest, puffing beeg cigar, enters my garden," he stormed. "No hello! 'Have you rooms?' he demands. 'How much?' 'For you, 300 euros,' I say, 'but we are booked up for years.' Ha! This is my house. You would not like people like that."

I was quite sure I wouldn't but wondered how I alone had been accepted, sight unseen; obviously, my Romanian friend had given me a good testimonial. I was reminded of the book that inspired this trip: Patrick Leigh Fermor's *Between the Woods and the Water*. In 1933, after being expelled from his English boarding school, he walked across Europe, from Rotterdam to Istanbul, alternately camping out and being taken in by local landowners as kind and eccentric as Constantin. His descriptions of Romania as a rustic paradise, unchanged in centuries, are deeply moving – all the more so because he was writing from memory, 50 years on.

Had this pastoral idyll been entirely swept away by the Nazi slaughter of gypsies and Jews, and half a century of barbarous rule from Bucharest? I feared it had but wanted to see for myself. I decided to avoid the big cities and focus on rural areas. There, villagers are still scything fields of hay, stacking it around tall poles, and riding home on horse-drawn carts through an intensely green landscape of meadows and mountains. Homeowners still commission richly carved wooden gates and create fretted tin canopies for wells they use every day. Looking beyond the abandoned factories and chaotic city centers, as well as the trickle of brash new mega-mansions and shiny black SUVs of the "beeg shots" Constantin had warned me about, I found much that Leigh Fermor would recognize from his youth, and a few marvels he missed on his leisurely trek.

Refreshing a painted barn

Sucevita Monastery church; Caveat for visitors

Detail of Last Judgment on west wall of Voronet Church

The monasteries around Gura Humor had long been on my wish list. I knew that the murals Giorgione and Carpaccio painted on Venetian palaces had vanished within a few decades. How could the monasteries have preserved their painted facades for 450 years? I set off down the road to the nearest of these, offered my 10 liu to a sweet-natured nun who had a few words of German, and shivered in anticipation. There, in an empty compound stood a church with broad eaves and a south front adorned with colors as intense as those of a medieval miniature, meticulously preserved under low light in a climate-controlled gallery at the Morgan Library in New York. Winter storms had bleached the apse and the north side, but the Tree of Jesse preserved the brilliant blue of lapis lazuli. The light was fading fast and I decided to get up early the next morning and visit all four in a single sweep.

Voronet, a few miles away, was the first and the most impressive. A hand-drawn sign warned against indecent dress, and I checked to be sure that my neck and arms were appropriately concealed. The penalties of sin are spelt out on the west wall, which is filled, side-to-side, with a Last Judgement. I lost what little faith my parents had instilled in me at age nine when I was thrown out of church choir in London for irreverence and unpunctuality (plus my inability to sing in tune). But I'm prepared to be awed by the efforts of artists to express the sacred and intimidate the gullible. As the English art critic Roger Fry observed, "Bach almost persuades me to be a Christian."

Here is a CinemaScope spectacle worthy of Cecil B. De Mille, but far livelier. Angels and devils contend for souls and the damned cascade down a great river of fire to hell. God is off-screen, but for a hand holding a scale. That's the main narrative, but, as in an illuminated manuscript, the artist has filled every cranny with exotic creatures as well as fanciful vignettes of marine life and opening graves. Sucevita is the grandest of the quartet, and there the theme of salvation is depicted in a Jacob's Ladder that extends across the north wall. The unlucky ones (no doubt including those who arrived in short shorts and with too much cleavage) tumble off the ladder into the arms of devils, the pious ones trudge on like health freaks at a gym, torturing themselves on a Stairmaster.

At Moldevita, the siege of Constantinople in 1453 is recast as a Christian victory over the Ottomans, but my enjoyment of this revisionist history was disturbed by a red-faced nun who was hectoring a party of tourists. Pointing to a scene of the Virgin ascending to heaven, she bellowed "Maria Himmelfahrt! Ja? Ja! Ja!" and continued, fortissimo, through

Spires and haystacks near the Ukrainian border

the entire panoply of miracles. I moved away and discovered that the west end of the church had been disfigured by vandals—mostly 19th-century Germans—who scrawled names over the murals. I silently wished that they, too, might be roasting in hell.

Driving from the north-east to the northwest corner of Romania takes you along the Ukrainian border, a frontier that all the car rental companies agree is verboten and which seems, in consequence, as chancy as the after-life in a medieval morality play. I went to the Marmures region in search of shingled wooden churches of the kind I admired in Norway and have long wanted to explore in Novgorod. Here, the bulbous domes of Orthodox churches are replaced by slender Gothic spires, rising from steeply-pitched roofs and flanked by pinnacles. The 150-foot spire of Surdesti is almost as graceful as that of Salisbury Cathedral in England, and was once the tallest wooden structure in Europe.

I sheltered from the rain under the gatehouse and a family emerged from the neighboring cottage: the son to sell me a ticket, the daughter to offer a hand-crafted model of the church, the mother to guide me through the claustrophobic interior. The spire is concealed by trees at the end of a muddy lane but reappears from afar, framed by haystacks in the surrounding meadows.

North of Baie Sprie, the road ascends through hilly country to Sighet. In Desesti, the church is set high above the village and framed by a flower-filled graveyard. The fence that surrounds it is punctuated by little shingled canopies, and crosses are submerged in the long grass. It was Sunday morning, and I hoped that the villagers would be wearing traditional dress. The women went partway, with pleated blouses, colorful headscarves, and wide skirts over layers of petticoats. The men were drab but sported silly straw hats that resembled flower pots.

Markers in the Merry Cemetery

Brancusi's Endless Column

I drove on to Sapanta to see the Merry Cemetery, an outdoor gallery of naïve art. Each marker portrays the deceased in life and, on the reverse side, at the moment of death. Stoves explode, miners are crushed by falling rocks, and there are many automobile accidents – no surprise to anyone who has experienced the auto da fe of Romanian highways. An obituary notice, irreverent in its candor, is posted below the portraits. A few boards replace earlier memorials – one shows a soldier being bayoneted during the first world war, another depicts a cavalry officer killed in 1944. Most are fresh-minted, but recall the traditional dress of an earlier era: black waistcoats, skirts and head scarfs for the women with their spindles; baggy white pants for the men with their scythes. However, the cast also includes an electronics repairman and a farmer with a shiny new tractor.

Another priority was the Endless Column, a masterwork by Constantin Brancusi. Romania's greatest artist spent most of his career in Paris, but returned in 1937 to create this extraordinary monument near the town of his birth. It was way off my route—more hours tailing trucks—but I arrived in the unpromising town of Targu Jiu with high expectations. "Wo ist der Brancusi?" I cried hoping that German would be understood, and was met with blank stares. Round the town I went, growing ever more anxious that the sculpture had been spirited away. I stopped at local stores and factory gates, and still there was no response. Finally, an old man strolled across, his wrinkled face creased in smiles. "Brancoush!" he declared (I had been pronouncing it incorrectly). "Du bist schön hier!" He pointed and there it was, in plain view: a stack of sixteen, gold painted steel rhomboids rising 100 feet from a circle of grass in a public park.

Romany dancers at the Szejeke Folk Festival

It's rare to encounter a legend you haven't seen in pictures, and this was one of those occasions. It was taller, slimmer, and more pristine than I had imagined. For an hour I stalked it, walking up to it and back and around, as locals gazed curiously at me – apparently a more interesting apparition. Visitors are few and that intensifies the sense of discovery that every traveler hopes for and seldom achieves. I knew a little of its history. The jagged profile was inspired by the carved-wood posts of this region, and Brancusi employed the same module as a base for many of his marble and bronze sculptures. The communists deplored its abstraction, and tried, unsuccessfully, to pull it down. Eight years ago it was restored with assistance from the Getty Conservation Institute. The column marks one end of an axis extending more than a mile across town to another park, where Brancusi carved an arch, rounded stools and a table from blocks of stone. I drove around, getting lost again, but knowing I'd accomplished the task that mattered.

To complete the circuit I drove back to Sighisoara, an impressive hill-top citadel that's being excavated for new sewers while energetically peddling the Dracula story and related souvenirs to tourists. Far more pleasing and unspoiled are the remoter villages that surround it. In the 12th century, when this was part of Hungary, the king invited industrious Saxons to settle the region, and they built fortified churches as refuges from Tatar and Turkish invaders.

I stayed in Biertan, one of the villages that has been reinvigorated by the Mihai Eminescu Trust, spending a couple of nights in a courtyarded house they rent to visitors. It is several miles off the main road and the church towers over the clustered red tile roofs. A wooden staircase ascends through three circuits of wall to a belvedere from which you can see nothing but the village and rolling hills. A neighbor came over to prepare dinner and left me in the stillness of whitewashed walls, bare floorboards, and a truckle bed. The loudest sounds next morning were clock chimes, the clip-clop of hoofs, and the lowing of cattle on the way to pasture.

The best surprise came on my last afternoon in Romania. Driving through Odorheiu Secuiesc on the road back to Sighisoara I spotted a banner announcing the Szejeke Folk Festival, and there, on the steps of the municipal theater were clusters of costumed dancers. I dashed inside; the first performance of the weekend was about to begin. The lighting was crude, the music mostly recorded. It didn't matter; the spectacle was electrifying. Dancers from Macedonia to the Ukraine swirled and spun their partners, skirts spinning like tops; the men kicking up their heels and slapping their knees.

Finally it was the turn of a Romany troupe and the families occupying the front rows snapped to attention. They stood and cheered as red-shirted men and gorgeously costumed women vied for supremacy, the harsh rhythms of the music driving them on, the tempo accelerating into an orgasmic explosion of color and motion. For a few moments, I was back in the vanished world Leigh Fermor brought so vividly to life.[2007]

FINLAND

Late on a cloudless afternoon in June, I went off to see Jari Jetsonen, an architectural photographer who lives in a village-like housing estate near the center of Helsinki. We chatted about his work and he invited me to stay for dinner and a sauna with his wife and three children. We gathered birch twigs in his garden to make switches, and, after an hour of steaming and a few cold beers I felt I was family, too.

Breaking the ice is what Helsinki is all about. Standing on one of the smooth granite outcrops that punctuate the city as emphatically as parking lots in LA, it's easy to visualize the glaciers that scoured this land a mere 10,000 years ago. Through the long dark winters huge icebreakers clear shipping lanes into the busy port. In the brief, brilliant summers, pale-skinned inhabitants sit outside until midnight, soaking up the last rays. Hot air balloons rise from Market Square and there is dancing in the streets to celebrate the end of hibernation.

I asked Antti Nurmesniemi, one of Finland's most prolific designers, about this craving for light, and he recalled a speech he gave in Paris. "I come from a land whose seasonal extremes influence our way of life," he told his audience. "I have my back to the icy rollers of the Arctic Ocean. Before me, Europe opens up like a huge garden, with the blue Mediterranean glittering in the distance."

Glass-blowing competition

Helsinki was merely a fortified port when the Russians seized Finland from the Swedes. They laid out a neoclassical city, a provincial version of St. Petersburg. A century later, the Finns expressed their longing for independence in romantic nationalist buildings that were inspired by medieval churches and farm buildings. Rusticated and carved granite facades with cupolas and turrets predominate in the waterfront neighborhoods of Katajonokka and Eira. Eliel Saarinen brought artistry to the style, joining two friends to create Hvitträsk, a villa just outside the city, and designing the imposing Central Station.

As Saarinen left to make a new life in America, Alvar Aalto launched his career as an organic architect of curvilinear walls and undulating wood vaults inspired by the forests and lakes. You can see his work while lunching at the Savoy restaurant, enjoying a concert in Finlandia Hall, or taking a tour of the National Pensions Institute. Aalto's mastery of fluid space, infused with natural light, is a tradition that lives on in the churches of Juha Leiviskä, and Steven Holl's Kiasma museum of contemporary art.

The craft tradition is alive and well. Timo Sarpaneva, the doyen of Finnish designers took me to the Great Nordic Glassblowing Contest, hosted in alternate years by Iitala and Orrefors. A row of barrel-chested men with faces as red as the open furnace took turns

Eliel Saarinen's Central Station, Helsinki

Steamer garlanded for midsummer night

blowing the largest dish, cylinder, or bubble from tiny knobs of molten glass. Lung-power expands the glittering prize, hands spin the pipe to maintain symmetry, but a faltering breath or a gust of wind from the open door can cause the glass to collapse like a punctured balloon. A row of small boys gazed up in awe from the side of the stage. At intermission, Timo was carried away by excitement and the succession of vodka toasts, leapt onto a table, and maintained his balance while making a rambling speech. His wife responded with sweet-toned songs in Finnish and Swedish, and a ribald English ditty in praise of schnapps.

In Helsinki, the countryside is never far away. A short tram ride brings you to a fretted wooden footbridge that leads to an outdoor museum on the island of Seurasaari. Rural buildings from all over Finland were brought here and scattered among the birch and pine trees. In summer, students in period costume guide you though the red stained timber houses and barns, but it's worth going just to stroll around this idyllic enclave that looks across the water to the center of the city.

Poor box at Seurasaari

Five million Finns inhabit a country that is only slightly smaller than Germany, and during the brief summer they migrate from towns to remote islands and lakefront cabins. The roads are almost empty, and I was able to drive around the southern third of the country without encountering more than a few cars and trucks. Everywhere I went there were stacks of fresh-cut logs, the scent of pine, and the glint of light off water. Wildflowers carpeted meadows of luminous green. One of the nicer surprises was a daily radio broadcast in Latin, presented as a public service by two classics professors. It sounded quite intelligible after hours of chatter in Finnish.

My Midsummer Night's Dream came aboard an old-fashioned lake steamer, decked with birch boughs, cruising around a shore where every village and weekend cottage had its celebratory bonfire. Flames flickered against a still brilliant sky, and rival steamers raced ours with a frantic blast of whistles and cheers from passengers lining the rails. In the following days, I explored painted wooden churches, windmills, and Poorvoo, the second oldest town in Finland and quite the prettiest. Brightly colored wooden houses cluster around the hilltop cathedral, and cobbled streets provide constantly shifting glimpses of fences, gables, and courtyards.

For every historic treasure, there was another work of Aalto, demonstrating his extraordinary versatility. In 1928, the Paimio Tuberculosis Sanatorium brought him international fame. I walked around the white stucco blocks and climbed the daffodil yellow staircases to admire the progressive furnishings, color accents, and broad balconies overlooking a forest. It felt more like a hotel than a hospital. The Villa Mairea of 1937 was built for his chief patron, Harry Gullichsen and his wife Mairea. It feels like a stylized forest with its wooden floors and ceilings, cane-wrapped columns and sculptured staircase. After the war, Aalto designed the all-brick town hall and library for the community of Saynätsälo. Turf-covered steps ascend to a council chamber that's dark and snug as a sauna. And last, the Church of the Three Crosses, a luminous white flower that seems to unfold as you walk through it.

A highlight of the trip was the Bonk Museum in Uusikaupunki. In a country that takes pride in its cutting-edge technology (Nokia was the Apple of that decade), a group of pranksters mounted an elaborate hoax: an exhibition of machines that never worked.

Monty Python might have hatched the plot. Around 1900 an inventor called Pare Bonk is supposed to have imported Peruvian anchovies, harnessed them to generate

Fanciful machine in the Bonk Museum

Aalto's Villa Mairea

electricity, and then ground them into a condiment he sold to the crowned heads of Europe. Riveted boilers and massive flywheels, dials, levers, and copper piping evoke the spirit of the Industrial Revolution. Attendants earnestly draw your attention to a fabricated page from the *Scientific American* extolling Bonk's inventions, and explain the functions of a dozen lovingly crafted engines. [1994]

DENMARK: COPENHAGEN

I'm sitting in the café of an art museum waiting for my club sandwich to arrive, which is hardly the kind of thing you write home about. But this is Copenhagen, and the sandwich is served with a flourish like the work of art it is: sliced chicken and braised red peppers with aioli on a bouquet of red-leaf lettuce atop a toasted slice of baguette, with another long slice poised above it like a jaunty hat brim on a long olive-tipped spear.

When I leave the lofty palm court of the Ny Carlsberg Glyptotek—a wonderfully ornate museum established about a century ago—I enter a recreation of a Roman temple, with stone columns and statuary, filled with sensuously curved plywood chairs, a 1950s classic by Arne Jacobsen. Next-door is the most beautiful modern staircase I've ever seen. Waxed plaster walls shimmer in the overhead light and shallow marble treads lead up and around a stack of new galleries. The architect was Henning Larsen, who has won a string of prestigious commissions, notably the imposing new opera house across the water from the royal palace.

My afternoon at the Glyptotek encapsulates what I love most about Copenhagen: a supremely self–confident city where old and new sit happily side by side, and even short-order cooks can be inventive. Design is embedded in the Danish DNA, infusing every aspect of daily life – from postage stamps to chairs, public transport to luxury hotels.

Tower of the Vor Freisers Kirke

Room 606 at the Radisson SAS Hotel

Fanciful copper spires and brick gables segue into impeccably detailed glass and steel boxes and no one protests that the city is being ruined as they do almost everywhere else when a new building is proposed for a historic district.

The Danish Design Center, a cool showcase for the best work of today adjoins the fairytale City Hall on Hans Christian Andersen Boulevard. The waterfront Admiral Hotel, where I stayed, is Terence Conran's sensitive remodel of an 18th-century granary, in which sharp modern furnishings complement stone arches and a forest of timber posts. To me, this juxtaposition of periods and styles is far more appealing than the cute, cuddly Copenhagen of the tourist brochures, which promote Tivoli Gardens, the Little Mermaid, and pedestrian shopping streets as the big attractions.

Copenhagen succeeds where other cities have failed, by maintaining a human scale. I picked up one of the city's free bicycles and wheeled off along one of the bike paths that line the broad boulevards. The pace was brisk, but not frenetic. There's none of the chaotic signage that clutters American streets, and even the new street lamps are aesthetic. The buildings maintain a consistent height so that spires and domes stand out from their neighbors, and there are no gaping holes for parking lots. The Queen lives in one of four elegant rococo mansions that flank the cobbled octagon of Amalienborg, and the only giveaway is the guard in period costume standing outside his kiosk.

I stopped to take a tour of the Radisson SAS Royal Hotel across from the railroad station. When it opened in 1960, it was Copenhagen's first high-rise and the flagship of Scandinavian Airlines, with a terminal in the base, an observation lounge at the top, and an elegant spiral stair linking the two levels of the lobby. Arne Jacobsen custom designed everything in it, from chairs to door handles and restaurant tableware. Room 606, the subject (and title) of a book, has been preserved in its original form, and I could have recreated it in my apartment, buying silverware at George Jensen, fabrics and furniture at Illums Bolighus or Paustian, and vintage items now out of production at one of the antique modern stores on Bredgade.

Anders Moesgard, a Copenhagen businessman, has done something of the kind at Bellevue – a complex of white stucco apartments that Jacobsen designed in the 1930s on a waterfront site just north of the city. When the housing and theater were recently restored, he took over the restaurant, named it for the architect, and put it back to its original condition. "It's a living museum," he says. "What makes me proudest is that Jacobsen's grandchildren often come to visit."

I rented a 10-speed bicycle to zip up the Strandvagen coastal road to Humlebaek, where another visionary, the late Knud Jensen, created the Louisiana museum of modern art. Jensen had a great love of the arts (he was close friends with the author Karen Blixen) and acquired a ruined estate with the goal of creating a new kind of museum – one that opened up to nature and would, as he explained, "exhibit the best and most controversial works of modern art, but in such a way that they didn't scare people." In 1956, he sold his business to Kraft Foods, and the profit enabled him to hire two young architects to create the first galleries, a cafeteria, and a sculpture garden looking out to the sea. Since then, Louisiana (named for the original owner's three successive wives, all of whom were named Louise) has grown to a circuit of galleries including one that is placed underground so as not to intrude on views of the sculpture garden.

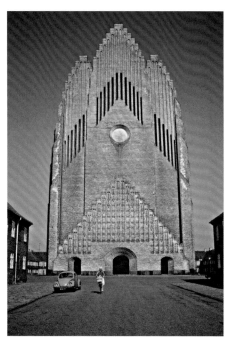

On the way back to the city, I stopped at Fredensborg, a village built around a royal palace, where Utzon designed a community of houses for returning foreign service officers. Low, yellow-brick cottages with

Grundtvigskirche looms over the neighboring community

shallow-pitched tile roofs wrap around leafy courtyards, and even as a stranger I felt at home and greeted residents as though I lived there. I felt equally welcome at Utzon's church in Bagsvaerd, where locals were straggling in for a Sunday service. Outwardly plain, the roof is as sensuously curved as the sails of the opera house. Concealed windows throw light over the undulating folds of whitewashed poured concrete, and skylights over the side galleries cast bars of shadow across the blond-wood benches.

Back in Copenhagen, I paused to see Grundtvigskirche, an even more remarkable church, which was built in 1940 as the centerpiece of a planned community. It resembles a jagged pyramid, looming over a village green and surrounded by tiny row houses built of yellow brick. I'm reminded of old prints that show medieval cathedrals dominating the skyline.

This is one of several architectural curiosities scattered through the city. The most cele-brated is the arched gateway to the Carlsberg Brewery with a pair of standing elephants on the outer face, and a reclining pair on the inside. The Thorvald Museum houses the neo-clas-sical statues of this famous Danish sculptor in a kind of Egyptian mausoleum, painted in soft tones of yellow and green. And what could be stranger than the Politgarden—an austere pentagonal block housing the city's good-tempered police—with its neo-classical circular courtyard? This would be the ideal location for Thorvald's heroically scaled figures—the police deserve a less intimidating structure—and his prettily painted museum could be recycled as a restaurant or a hotel.

I returned to the Admiral, and a scrumptious dinner of rabbit with rhubarb, and venison with asparagus in Salt, a restaurant built around the massive timbers that withstood a bombardment by the British fleet, two centuries ago. Now the only vessels close by are the vast Norway ferry and a graceful American yacht, the *Ragusa*, which sailed across the Atlantic from Bristol, RI, to participate in the Cowes regatta, and continue on to the Baltic. The crew stow the sails, lower the stars and stripes, and leave the lean hull and towering mast as their temporary contribution to the city

Ann Videriksen, a Danish architect who has joined me for dinner, tries to explain why her countrymen are so caught up in design. "We were fortunate in being so poor after the war," she suggests. "Frugality became a way of life. We are a small country, with few natural resources besides our wits, and the move from agriculture to industry didn't come until the 1940s. So we are still in touch with our roots."

In the taxi to the airport, I asked the driver who his favorite architect was and why. Not only had he heard of Jacobsen, Utzon, and Larsen, but he knew and liked some of their build-ings. Try asking a question like that the next time you ride to Kennedy or O'Hare. [2003]

AERO

Aero: main square of Aerøskøbing

A perfect day on the enchanting island of Aero. Lush fields extend to the narrow, rocky beaches—I never found a sandy shore—and tiny, colorful beach houses line the spits of land stretching out from the two major towns with some trees and small hills, but mostly low-lying, looking over placid waters to coastlines that barely mark the horizons. To wake up at the Pension Vestergade is a delight. The house is dated 1784, a tall gabled brick block with six double rooms and separate bathrooms opening off white corridors. The breakfast room opens onto a long, green garden with two small summerhouses; next-door is the library. Susanna, who is English and married to a Dane, has been managing the pension for 14 years and obviously loves the job.

The house is at the mid-point of Vestergade, the best street in the town of Aerøskøbing, which won the Europa Nostra prize in 2001 for the quality of its architecture and preservation. The cobbled streets curve, giving them a feeling of enclosure. Each house is two or three stories, but different in shape, color, and ornament, achieving a harmonious ensemble. There are a few parked cars, but little commerce. The main square is quite plain; the whitewashed church with its squat black spire lies behind. Wildflowers are painted on the ends of the misty blue pews, and ship models are suspended between the chandeliers. Apparently a major speculator ruined the economy of Aerøskøbing in the 1850s and the town went to sleep.

I drove to Marstall to meet Karsten at the Maritime Museum. He's a tall, buoyant man who runs the museum, is church organist, local historian, and mounts a summer opera production with singers from the Royal Opera. This year it's *La Bohème*: one performance for an audience of 650 in a warehouse with excellent acoustics. The museum is a delight: a warren of

Maritime Museum in Marstall

rooms in two adjoining houses, each crammed with ship models, paintings, charts, and assorted memorabilia, including exotic finds from distant countries, all donated by the seamen of Marstall. At its peak, Marstall had a population of 5,000 and around 350 ships that carried salted cod to Portugal and Spain, Brazil and West Africa, as well as the northern seas up to Murmansk. It was the second largest port in Denmark after Copenhagen. We looked around, admiring the extraordinary collection of model ships in bottles, painstakingly crafted by men with large calloused hands. A white-bearded veteran restores the rigging of the larger models. Across the street a whole ship, once lost, was being restored for a voyage to Newfoundland. [2010]

Stockholm: Gamla Stan

Romeo & Juliet ballet in City Hall courtyard

Cruising around the waterfronts of Stockholm on a fine summer's day is one of the most civilized pleasures I know. The city covers 14 islands of varied size, a tiny part of the archipelago of 24,000 rocky outcrops that extends from Lake Malaren out into the Baltic. The water acts as a giant mirror, intensifying the cool northern light, and enhancing the fanciful skyline. The islands break up the mass of the city, giving it an intimacy and charm that belies its size. Monuments—including the landmark City Hall and a forest of church spires—stand out boldly from streets and promenades of uniform scale and height. The cobbled lanes of the old city frame views of other islands, leafy parks, and an animated mix of ferries and sail boats. Though Stockholm has an abundance of restrained modern buildings, it preserves the rich character of earlier centuries in which architects competed to impress.

Copper Tent in Haga Park, near Drottingholm

A short walk over the bridges to the north and west takes you past the House of the Nobility (Riddarhuset) a triumph of the baroque with its giant Corinthian pilasters and graceful copper roof, and on to City Hall, the finest monument of the last century. Its tall corner tower has a fanciful lantern topped with three crowns, and they are echoed in turrets that protrude from the tall, brick walls. It's a hybrid of the National Romantic style that flourished in Scandinavia in the early 1900s, and the clean lines and bare surfaces of modernism. The mosaic-lined Golden Hall, where the Nobel Prize ceremony is held, was inspired by St. Mark's Basilica in Venice.

I crossed the bridge to the irregular oval of Skeppsholmen. Rafael Moneo's Museum of Modern Art has one of the finest collections of 20th-century paintings and sculptures in Europe and the architectural museum also presents lively exhibitions. A ferry carried me to the waterfront Vasa Museum, a soaring modern container for the royal flagship that capsized and sank on her maiden voyage in 1628. The richly carved hull was raised and restored 50 years ago and you view it close-up at different levels. A short walk inland brings you to Skansen, the word's first open-air museum of rural life and a model for those that have followed. Farm buildings, churches, a manor house, and a village school were brought here from all over Sweden, plus wild and domestic animals, transporting city folk to a pastoral world that still survives in remoter parts of the country. Another ferry carries you back to the central square of Nybroplan, past the palatial facades of Strandvagen.

There's a design store named for the architect, Gunnar Asplund, who designed two of the city's masterworks. The Public Library is a lofty book-lined rotunda of the 1920s, and Skogskyrkogarden, which translates as Woodland Cemetery, is a serene enclave with a modest chapel. It was Asplund's last great work, completed in 1940, and is now a UNESCO World Heritage site.

When I'd had my fill of the city, I took the hour-long boat ride along peaceful waterways to Drottningholm, also a UNESCO site. There you can explore the baroque palace that is the principal residence of the otherwise unpretentious royal family, wander across the park to the fanciful Chinese Pavilion (commissioned by the king as a surprise for his consort in 1753), and detour to Haga Park to see the Turkish-style copper tent. After dinner at an open-air restaurant came an opera in a replica of the court theater where Ingmar Bergman made his enchanting film version of Mozart's *The Magic Flute*. To sustain the spell, I sailed back to Stockholm through the softly glowing twilight. [2003]

Maypole at Skansen

NORWAY

A narrow road snakes up the side of a mountain, making nine hairpin turns before reaching the summit. Silver threads of water course down the rock face, merging into cascades that swell a rushing stream. The road is bounded with lichened rocks and embraced by pines and silver birches. At the top a steel walkway cantilevers out to provide an overhead view of the road, snow-dappled peaks, and the green valley beyond. This is Trollstigen, a place of wonder in central Norway.

No other European country can offer such spectacles. The prices are high, the strictly enforced speed limits are low, and the weather is erratic, but the rewards far outweigh these deficiencies. Mountains rise steeply from deep fjords, and every journey is a succession of winding roads, tunnels, and ferries. Ibsen's Norway of poverty and puritan gloom has given way to an oil-fueled economy that is pouring money into infrastructure and social services.

The hairpin turns of the Trollstingen Road

A few coastal cities are booming, and mobs of tourists descend from giant cruise ships, but the countryside is still pristine. For the super-fit, it's a fantastic opportunity to hike, bike, and (for six months in the year) ski cross-country. The midnight sun can be as elusive as the Northern Lights in winter, but the days are long from May through September, and mist— even rain—can add a layer of mystery to the vistas as it does in Japan. And, in contrast to Japan, the five million inhabitants are mostly fluent in English, and their long isolation has left a legacy of warmth and friendliness.

The Norwegian road authority has commissioned architect-designed overlooks along 18 of the most spectacular routes, over the 1,000 miles from north to south, and a circuitous week-long drive from Oslo to Trondheim, Bergen and back provides a good sampling of varied architecture and fantastic landscapes. Plotting a route that takes in the best spots is a challenge because they are widely scattered, but the detours pay off and everything is well signposted.

Driving north from Oslo to Roros, a former mining town that is now a UNESCO World Heritage Site, you can linger to explore two extraordinary museums designed by Sverre Fehn, Norway's greatest modern architect. Hedmark is built atop the stone ruins of a medieval bishop's palace. The exterior is plain, but the interior is brilliantly recreated: a handsome wood vault atop the ruined stone walls, poured concrete ramps extending through and out to the courtyard, and a concrete deck and niches for period artifacts, secular and sacred. There's a wonderful interplay of architecture, machinery, and antiques. Aukrustsenteret in Alvdal celebrates the work of an eccentric local artist. From there, a side road loops past the Sohlbergplassen overlook, with its thrilling panorama of mountains, water, and forest.

I spent a night at the Juvet Landscape Hotel, an ideal fusion of nature and contemporary design, located just beyond Trollstigen. Nine wood cabins, with Zen minimal interiors, are scattered through forested landscapes, each framed by a wall of glass. Owner

Borgund stave church

Knut Slinning welcomed me to a dinner of local produce in an old red barn, and offered advice on expeditions. Heading south, there's a short detour to the medieval stave church of Borgund, a newly-restored masterpiece of wood construction, before continuing on to Aurland, a village that clings to the edge of a fjord. The longest road tunnel in the world carries the E 16 highway through the mountains, or you can climb over them on the old route 243, traversing a lunar landscape of granite scoured by glaciers. The ultimate reward is the Stegastein overlook: a laminated wooden walkway that ends in a balustrade of glass before dropping as sharply as a waterfall. From here, Aurland resembles a toy village and the boats seem like tiny models.

On the road to the Lofotens

It feels as though you had stepped into a landscape painting, but down below, reality awaits. Norwegians don't flaunt their newfound wealth, but they love to indulge their hobbies, and one of these is driving exotic cars. A hundred vintage MG roadsters, tops down, rallied on the mountain road, and eight vintage Corvettes, impeccably restored, were lined up outside the Fjord Hotel. They added another element to a scene that has changed little in the past century.

I flew to the northern city of Bodo and took the car ferry to the Lofoten islands, an archipelago that's linked by one-lane bridges. It's located north of the Arctic Circle, but warmed by the Gulf Stream, so the temperature never goes much below zero. In early June it was a chilly 40 degrees, though I was told that May was the hottest ever recorded, with temperatures as high as 80. I stayed at the Finnholmen Brygge, a red-boarded inn overlooking the harbor of Henningsvaer. The deep inlet is lined with wooden houses set at angles--red, green, yellow, and orange--and a large white cube that was once a caviar processing plant and is now an art gallery.

I spent the next several days exploring the islands, heading south to Å and another village called Bø, but I was unable to find C-Z. The Lofotens are a popular resort in high summer, and there are the inevitable tourist attractions. Nusfjord is a smartly painted village that charges admission, and the Lofotr Viking Museum is located on the site of a chieftain's hall. Visitors can row a long boat on the lake, and engage in a multitude of entertainments.

Away from those and a couple of towns, I reveled in the lonely expanse of water and sheer slopes, with a narrow road snaking between. The landscape is a mix of inlets and rocky islets; mountains, tumbled rocks richly encrusted with lichens, and granite screes scoured smooth by glaciers. The lower slopes are covered with moss and wild flowers, but trees are rare. Four-fifths of the world's cod come here to spawn and Lofoten is a major producer of stock

Fishermen's cottages; Nordic light in the Lofoten Islands

fish, which is exported to Southern Europe. Cod-drying frames are ubiquitous, though they stand empty in summer. A succession of fishing villages hug the inlets, each with its wood boathouses on stilts or perched on rocks, painted dark red or yellow ochre, with white trim.

Ulf Gronvold, a new friend in Oslo, gave me an introduction to his son Jens who, at age 30, is priest of five parishes (jointly with a lesbian who lives with her partner) and an avid outdoorsman. We talked of everything but religion, but I showed a keen appreciation for the succession of churches he showed me, from the intimate space at Kabelvag to the cavernous wooden Gothic cathedral. Flakstad is built of logs with a graceful baroque spire, and the obligatory model ship suspended amid modern chandeliers. A spare white church has twice been toppled by hurricanes and is now braced with steel cables on the landward side since the storms come over the mountains, not from the sea. Jens grew up in Oslo, and spent time in India and Mexico, before accepting this job because priests are paid substantially more to work in the north. Now he appreciates the natural beauty, the challenge of mountaineering, and the bond he has established with his flock.

On my last night, I booked dinner at the Brygge Hotel in Henningsvaer. The waitress apologized that the menu had been curtailed for a lack of kitchen staff; all she could offer was whale – carpaccio, or braised with boiled potatoes. I was reminded of the Monty Python sketch in which a hapless diner is informed that there is nothing to order but rook.

While considering whether to set aside my prejudices or stalk out, deliverance came from the man at the next table. As a director of the hotel he had authority, and recommended lamb (which proved delicious) and offered a very good St. Emilion as an apology. The Swedish chef, who had cooked in England, added some smoked salmon and rhubarb sorbet with salted nuts. It was quite the best dinner of the trip. [2013]

NETHERLANDS

In Amsterdam, historic and modern buildings coexist in harmony, and daring additions enhance storied landmarks. There's a spectacular new atrium to accommodate the crowds that flock to see the Rembrandts and Vermeers in the Rijksmuseum, and many of the galleries have been redesigned to enhance the collection of medieval and Renaissance arts and, in the furthest room, a vintage airplane. The florid brick Stedelijk Museum, which has always pushed the boundaries of art and design, has expanded into a giant white bathtub. Traditionalists were shocked, but the addition provides two new floors of galleries for temporary exhibitions, a canopied glass

Dutch modernism: Open-Air School, Amsterdam

foyer looking out to the Museumplein, and a spacious café-restaurant.

The courtyard of the Scheepsvartmuseum—an 18th-century naval store turned maritime museum—has been enclosed by a glass canopy supported on a delicate steel spider's web. Central Station, a neo-Renaissance landmark, has been remodeled with a new bus station to the rear, and, close by, a gorgeous Art Nouveau shipping office has been transformed into the Grand Hotel Amrâth. Architect Hubert-Jan Henket showed me how he had restored the Beurs van Berlage, a former exchange building that now hosts art exhibitions and trade fairs.

Zonestraal, Hilversum

The 17th- and 18th-century gabled houses that line the canals were revolutionary in their day – for their rationality, plain facades, and expansive windows. The pulleys that hoisted heavy loads to upper-level workshops are still used to raise a piano or sofa to an upstairs apartment. That spirit of innovation was revived a century ago by a brilliant generation of architects, artists, and designers, making the Netherlands a major center of modernism. Housing societies sponsored some of the best living complexes in the world, using brick with expressive freedom, and incorporating landscaped courtyards. The 1930 Open-Air School has been restored and brings joy to a new generation of children. It's one of many public buildings that embody the idealism of a society that sought to improve the lives of the many rather than enrich a few.

Amsterdam is growing rapidly, and a new city is wrapped around the historic core. Land is precious (a third of the country lies below sea level) so the density of these new developments is high. Large apartment buildings open onto the waterfront or a network of canals in the former docklands and factory sites. In a city that is as flat as a billiard table, it's easy to rent a bicycle to explore these new districts, hopping on and off free ferries or pedaling over the bridges that link them. That will take you to the Eye Film Institute, across the water from the station, a jagged white dart that contains a multiplex, a museum of cinema, and a restaurant that opens onto the water.

A network of storied cities, easily reached by train from Amsterdam, boast the same inspiring mix of old and new. Utrecht is a pilgrimage site for admirers of Gerrit Rietveld, who designed the red-blue chair and the Schröder-Schräder house, a tiny masterpiece of De Stijl. You can also visit a little-known gem that was inspired by Rietveld: a triangular house that Mart van Schijndel designed for himself in 1991 and shoehorned onto a hidden site once occupied by stables. It's maintained by his widow, Natascha Drabbe, who gives regular

Former post office, Utrecht

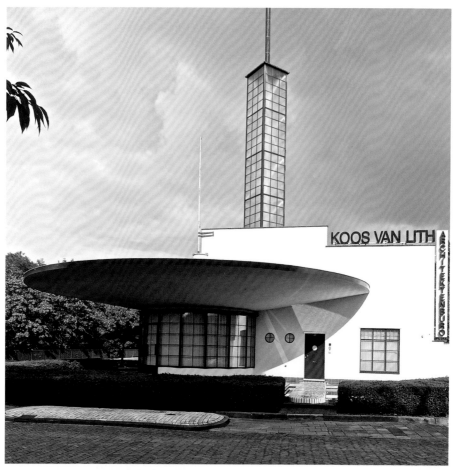

Former gas station, now an architect's office, Nijmegen

tours and launched the Iconic Houses association to protect and promote other modern house-museums in Europe and the US. The post office will soon have a new role as a public library and the main hall is as grand as a cathedral with its arched vault of glazed yellow bricks, ribbed glass, and black statuary.

Close to Utrecht is Hilversum, with the yellow brick City Hall of Willem Dudok, and Jan Duiker's Zonnestraal Sanatorium, a poetic interplay of gleaming white orthogonal blocks and rounded bays, subtly overlaid, and linked by spiral staircases. Both have been impeccably restored as time capsules of progressive architecture around 1930. The city was once a hub of European broadcasting, and that legacy is celebrated in the striking Institute for Sound and Vision, which doubles as a museum and an archive.

Away from the bustle of Dutch cities, served by a network of railways and gleaming new stations, is the pastoral landscape that painters celebrated: grazing cows, still canals, clusters of trees and a huge cloud-dappled sky. On a misty September morning I drove out from a rural B&B to the National Park de Hoge Veluwe. This expanse of woods and dunes was the private estate of Anton and Hélène Kröller-Müller, who bequeathed the land and their extraordinary art collection to the nation in the 1930s. The sober brick museum that Henry van der Velde designed in 1938 is as unpretentious and open to nature as Louisiana in Denmark, and the art is as good and varied as in almost any metropolitan institution.

A scarlet X of red-painted steel by Mark di Suvero emerged from the lawn like a giant asterisk, evidence that the museum has continued to collect, 80 years after the death of its founder. I had expected crowds on this fine Sunday, but I had the place almost to myself. In Amsterdam's Van Gogh Museum, a row of heads block every painting; here, a room of his masterpieces was deserted for the first 15 minutes, and I experienced the same ecstatic delight as I had, many years ago, in solitary communion with the Botticellis in room 8 of the Uffizi. Moments like this are increasingly rare – an opportunity to enter the soul of a great artist and savor every brushstroke.

Van Gogh was Hélène's favorite painter, but her tastes ranged from peasant art to Cubism and Futurism. There's a marvelous monochromatic Juan Gris (Bottle and Knife) that I would give everything I possess to own; a fine Seurat of Parisian cabaret dancers; a Balla screen, and a hundred other works of note in small top-lit galleries that open up diagonal axes and views into the inner courtyard.

I wandered outside, pausing at the pavilion that Gerrit Rietveld added in the 1950s: planes of concrete block that seem to slide past each other and frame bronzes by Henry Moore and Barbara Hepworth. The sculpture garden is idyllic – classic modern pieces widely spaced on smooth lawns (ravaged by moles) amid pools and mature trees. A hazy sun emerged and the whole scene shimmered. A restaurant is housed in a peaked tent open at the sides and serves a very good salmon salad. Guards cycle around, and that would be the ideal way to explore this 600-acre garden, as I did at Versailles long ago. I'm too wobbly to do that now, but—no matter—I had seen enough for one day. Less is more. [2013/17]

Sculpture Park of the Kröller-Müller Museum

Zabriskie Point

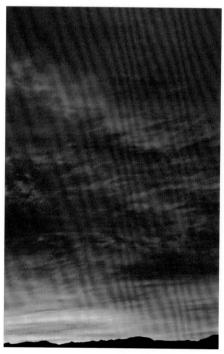

Sunset over Furnace Range

Spectacular canyons, mesas and deserts are scattered though the western states, but Death Valley tops them all – for its diversity and surreal beauty. Mountains overlook salt flats that are the lowest point in the US. The whole valley was once part of an inland sea; now it's one of the driest places on Earth. It earned its name from the pioneers who had to cross it on their way to California; many died of heat or exhaustion, and it can still be a lethal place in summer. Prospectors came in search of gold, lured by the polychrome mineral outcrops, but none was found.

I first went there in February, driving from LA with friends, and staying at Stove Pipe Wells Village. The approach raised our expectations: a shimmering tilted perspective of the Panamint Mountains. Winter rains had caused the desert to bloom, and the flats were carpeted in wildflowers. The dunes were sharp-etched in the late afternoon light, traced with windblown ripples and tracks of the tiny animals that find shelter there. We left at dawn the next day to watch the sun rise over Zabriskie Point, an otherworldly expanse of beige mud hills, cascading down to a dried riverbed. The ribs were deeply shadowed, creating a wonderful chiaroscuro.

We drove through 20-Mule Canyon (named for the wagons that transported borax) and up to Dante's View for a panorama of rocky bluffs, flats, and snow-capped mountains. Whenever we stopped the car, the silence rang in our ears as a tangible presence; nothing and nobody disturbed the stillness.

A detour brought us to Death Valley Junction, a white arcaded square that felt as unreal as a movie set. There was a small hotel, the Opera House—a quixotic one-woman venture—and an emporium that called itself "the most unique boutique in the desert." I asked the boy behind the counter how it was in summer. "Kinda warm," he admitted. The only other inhabitants in view were a couple of men playing guitar and fiddle for their

Musicians at Death Valley Junction

own pleasure. Just beyond the square was a wreckers' yard, full of dreamboats that had succumbed like the early settlers. In the blaze of midday every tangled mass of paint and chrome was as sharply defined as a John Chamberlin sculpture. [1973]

Sand dunes

GHOST TOWN

Bodie, a ghost town in a state of arrested decay

At first sight, Bodie resembles an engraving, fly specked and brown with age. The most substantial and authentic of California's many ghost towns, it evokes the frenzy of the Gold Rush and the slow decay of the Great Depression. Dark pine shacks, some tilted, others skeletal, straggle across an eastern slope of the Sierra Nevada. On the bluff behind the town are piles of turned earth and a cluster of mine buildings. Walk closer and you'll find rusty engines and boilers, wagon wheels and the shell of a 1930s automobile scattered through the grass.

The weathered tin on roofs and walls glows ruddily as the sun drops behind the mountains. Late in the day, when most visitors have left, the only sounds are of creaking timber and metal flapping in the constant wind. Every turn reveals another relic. You can just make out the sign of La Belle beauty parlor, and a long-defunct hotel that offered rooms and meals at all hours. Strips of canvas wave like a tattered banner. Shadows lengthen, and the deserted streets come alive with the phantoms and echoes of Bodie's raucous past.

At its peak, around 1880, nearly 10,000 hopefuls lived here, but the boom was short-lived. The barren plateau is more than 8,000 feet high and you can imagine how desolate it must have seemed to the first settlers. But the lure was irresistible. In the first three years, mines yielded $100 million in ore. Miners earned $4 a day and squandered their wages on whisky, gambling, and good-time girls. A preacher described the town as "a sea of sin lashed by the tempests of lust and passion." A young girl wrote in her diary, "Good-bye God, I'm going to Bodie." A hardy few lingered on as mining waxed and waned until, by the late 1940s, only a caretaker was left. In the ensuing years, Bodie was ravaged by storms, fires, and vandals until, in 1962, it was made a State Historic Park. Three rangers live on site to protect the remaining 170 buildings and maintain them in a state of arrested decay.

The mementos of humble lives are strangely moving. A Dodge-Graham truck is parked beside two hand-operated gas pumps; you can imagine the Joad family emerging from the general store and resuming their creaky passage from the Oklahoma dust bowl to the promised land of California's Central Valley. Inside the schoolhouse, instructions and sums are chalked on the blackboard, and map shows the world as it was just before the first World War. You wait for the kids to return for the books they left on their desks. [1992]

CONCOURS D' ELEGANCE

A Concours d'Elegance has been held on the Pebble Beach golf course in California every year since 1950. Aficionados get up before dawn to witness the parade of legendary marques emerging from the sea mist and chugging or gliding, smoking or steaming to their appointed places. I was lucky enough to join them, in company with Charlie Sholvay, a collector who races a 1926 Bugatti. Most contenders date from the first four decades of the last century, and the forms are as exotic as the names, for these cars were hand-made in workshops, one at a time. Duesenbergs and duPonts, Hispano-Suizas and Pierce-Arrows, Delages and Delahayes, Bugattis and Lagondas were custom built for moguls, maharajas, and movie stars, with liveried chauffeurs to buff and park these monsters. The parade also features scores of Packards and a sprinkling of Cords, along with a few classic brands that have survived bankruptcies and corporate mergers.

Stately or streamlined, each of these lovingly restored automobiles is a work of art assembled from sculptured hoods, sweeping fenders and trunks that often conceal a rumble seat and support one or a pair of spare tires, for punctures were frequent on unpaved roads. Everything is separately delineated: spring-loaded bumpers, massive headlights,

Concours d'Elegance: Hispano-Suiza 1925

Kissel Kar 1912

trumpet-like horns and—most covetable and distinctive—hood ornaments. Like the armorial bearings of chivalry, these mascots were proudly flaunted and a few became as famous as the cars they adorned. These classics make me deeply covetous and it's just as well that only millionaires can afford to restore and maintain them or I might be tempted to plunge. My 1968 Mustang convertible occupies middle ground between style and practicality and, as long as it runs smoothly I'll resist the lure of European sirens and vintage chariots. Look but don't touch, as owners tell the admiring throng. [1999]

HIGH DESERT HOUSE, JOSHUA TREE

The High Desert House near Palm Springs is the masterpiece of Kendrick Bangs Kellogg, an organic architect who draws inspiration from nature and from his mentor, Frank Lloyd Wright. Beginning in 1957 at age 23, he created a succession of houses and commercial buildings that shape space in daring ways, but his originality condemned him to obscurity. Like the late John Lautner, another protegé of Wright, he cannot be readily categorized and has thus been largely ignored by editors and critics. As a maverick in his ninth decade, he craves recognition and the opportunity to build but proudly refuses to compromise his vision.

Kellogg's last great project was commissioned by two artists, who found a site perched among sandstone boulders, overlooking Joshua Tree National Monument. The architect conceived a giant flower of overlapping concrete petals that enclose a soaring open space, an elevated master bedroom, and a downstairs guest suite. The structure seems to grow out of the boulders like the spiky Joshua trees that give this expanse of wilderness its name. Construction stretched out over many years, and the rough-textured shell was then enriched for another two decades by John Vugrin, a craftsman of rare skill from San Diego. Etched glass, sinuously

Ken Kellogg's High Desert House

curved marble, wood, and bronze define an open work area, a sunken sitting room, dining area, kitchen, and bathrooms. The pool terrace was transformed into a glass-enclosed spa.

Chance played a large role in the creation of this extraordinary house. Jimmy and Beverley Doolittle acquired the four-hectare site in exchange for a flat plot on the street that would have been much easier to build on. They saw several of the houses Kellogg had built in San Diego and invited him to drive up to Joshua Tree. He chose the ridge as the ideal location, then sketched an open, light-filled space on a yellow pad. Aerial photographs were combined with land surveys to create a site model as the plans grew from the initial concept. Little did the Doolittles realize what they were embarking on. To describe the experience, they quote a line from science-fiction author Ray Bradbury: "you jump off a cliff and build your wings on the way down."

No contractor would assume responsibility for such an audacious design in so remote a location. Instead, the owners hired a supervisor and paid him for time and materials, without setting a deadline. A team of unskilled workers figured out solutions as they went along. It took three years to cut the rock, lay a concrete pad, and construct a driveway, while leaving many of the boulders in place. Twenty-six hollow columns are deeply rooted in the rock and fan out to form the overlapping planes that block the sun, while admitting refracted light through the glazed spaces between. Steel and concrete withstand the desert climate much better than wood, and neoprene joints allow the glass to expand. Terraces extend out to either side, shaded and protected by the house from fierce desert winds. There's an architectural promenade from the road, up a winding paved path, and through the interior spaces to the wall of rocks behind. The house is a place of grandeur and mystery; a total work of art, seamlessly fused with nature at its most sublime.

From the rusted steel fence and a gate that resembles a dinosaur skeleton to the ornamental

Living area of the High Desert House

drain covers and portcullis-like front door, Vugrin's craftsmanship is everywhere apparent. His sculptural exuberance and love of ornament rival those of Gaudí. He fabricated almost everything--from furniture, hand basins, etched glass, and built-ins to copper light switches. Two cast-bronze beams arch down through the living area to support glass work surfaces. Shifting levels define the different areas of the house but there are very few doors, and each space flows smoothly into the next. The master bedroom is elevated and encircled with pleated, backlit translucent glass so that the cylindrical form hovers, like a gigantic lantern, within the main space. A sunken seating area at its base is warmed by a hearth inset with smooth pebbles and a snail-like copper hood. The master bathroom is sculpted from marble and bronze, and a shower is set beside the boulders and natural spring to the north. The juxtaposition of different materials and textures, rough and smooth, raw and refined, animates every corner.

There is a constantly shifting play of light and shadow through the day. At an elevation of 4,000 feet, far from the nearest city, the air is piercingly clear, and the sun beats down fiercely. The house filters its beams, creating a penumbra of light that throws every surface into relief. Early and late, when the sun is low, its rays softly model the petals of the roof canopy from below. At high noon it is held at bay and hot air is evacuated through vents in the glazing. There's a dramatic contrast between the mass of the shelter and the openness of the stone-paved terraces, blurring the boundary between indoors and outdoors in a way that's hard to achieve in the desert valleys, where summer temperatures soar to 120 degrees, and residents retreat into air-conditioned cocoons. The High Desert House is a sustainable response to climatic extremes. [2013]

TIPPET RISE, MONTANA

Tippet Rise, looking towards the Beartooth Mountains

Domo, a concrete structure that serves as a sounding board for live music

Barely a million people live in Montana—a state that is larger than Germany—and most are concentrated in a few cities. That allowed Peter and Cathy Halstead's foundation to assemble a ranch of 125,000 acres from 13 summer pastures and create Tippet Rise, a unique stage for the arts. Inspiration came from Storm King Sculpture Park in mid-state New York and music festivals around the world, but the Halsteads were also determined to preserve and enhance the extraordinary beauty of the grasslands and canyons that roll away to the Beartooth Mountains. To the south is Yellowstone National Park with its geysers, rushing streams, wolves, and bison. As the state license plates proclaim, this is Big Sky Country.

Four architectural firms were invited to compete for new structures, but their proposals seemed too conventional, and the choice fell on Ensamble, the Madrid-Boston firm headed by Antón García-Abril and his wife Débora Mesa. They became part of the team, designing a series of cast concrete structures that would reflect sound and serve as markers in the landscape. Domo, largest of the three that have been realized thus far, shelters recitals for audiences of a hundred or more.

Tippet Rise is a cultural resource for residents and a destination for arts lovers, who fly to Billings, drive at great speed on the interstate freeway, slow down on winding roads and trails, before coming to rest behind a grassy berm. They glimpse the roof of a barn, clad in Corten, rising beside a black steel Calder stabile. The Olivier Music Barn is a masterpiece of understatement—warm, reverberant, and luminous—providing ideal acoustics for performers as well as an audience of 150 on director chairs and wall benches.

Site-specific art works—by Patrick Dougherty, Stephen Talasnik, and two heroically-scaled steel constructions by Mark di Suvero—are strategically positioned off the eight-mile trail that leads to Domo. This is a three-legged monolith, which grew from the seed of Truffle, a tiny guest cabin of roughly poured concrete that Ensamble created near Santiago de Compostella in 2008. That first experiment was conceived as a dialogue between architecture and nature, rooted in the land. The tilted slabs of Inverted Portal and Beartooth Portal develop that idea, serving as markers in the much grander expanse of Tippet Rise. Domo is part structure, part sculpture, evoking a rock outcrop, carved and polished by wind and water. The western deserts are full of such natural phenomena, and Ensamble have channeled their organic shapes and textures.

Architecture that engages the landscape enriches the experience of music-making and art, attracting a wide range of talent and loans from major museums. Tippet Rise is open to the public four days a week for hiking and tours in electric vans. The first seven weekends of music were sold out, mostly to locals, and programming is likely to expand in the years to come. Ensamble have planned an ambitious new structure, and there will be more art works and educational activities. For the Halsteads, this is the culmination of a lifetime of travel, creativity, and support for the arts. She paints, he has played piano since he was five (though his father hated music and turned his first piano into a desk while the boy was away at school). Now he collects vintage Steinways, including Vladimir Horowitz's favorite, and the hills of Montana are alive with the sound of music. [2016]

Strathmore Apartments: shaded deck

BACK HOME

This memoir began with the briefest of journeys, from bed to air-raid shelter, and it ends with my daily peregrinations. For the past 40 years I've lived in a hilltop apartment that Richard Neutra designed in 1937, the year I was born. Eight units enclose a steeply sloping courtyard. Dense plantings conceal a classic modern composition of white blocks with flat roofs and ribbon windows, so that my apartment feels like a tree house. The 64, steep steps that lead up from the street to my door afford privacy and some relief from the noise of traffic and reveling students, though not from the helicopters that zoom in to the UCLA Medical Center at all hours. I should be grateful they are not blasting "Ride of the Valkyries." Most of the time it's peaceful and I can sit out on my terrace, entertaining friends or reading, while gazing out over a densely layered neighborhood. Living well is the best revenge, and now I've turned 80, I feel profoundly grateful that I've spent half my life in this enchanted aerie.

The architect Craig Hodgetts introduced me to the Strathmore apartments, showing me the unit just vacated by Larry Gagosian, who was moving to a house-gallery Craig had designed in Venice. It was too close to the street for my taste, so I recommended it to a friend who was almost deaf. Six months later she told me the top unit was free, and I grabbed it. I spent the next decade camping out with a minimum of furnishings, leaving doors and windows open for most of the year. The abundance of light and good proportions were enough in themselves – a blessed release from the claustrophobia of an old dark house in DC. The 1994 earthquake spared the apartment and spurred me to celebrate my household gods, Neutra and the Eameses.

Neutra designed the project to generate revenue during the Great Depression. Prospective renters shied away, muttering "moon architecture," and the architect was lucky to find a compatriot, actress Luise Rainer, as his first tenant. She had won two best-actress Oscars back-to-back, and was splitting from her husband, Clifford Odets. Neutra furnished the living room with built-in bookshelves and Venetian blinds, just as I have done, and invited Julius Shulman to photograph the two of them together.

In return, she wrote to the architect, telling him that she had always been afraid of modernism, thinking it cold and unfriendly, but now "the clearness, the long lines of windows which allow the light to come in and the eye to rove out far, far; all of this gives you a strange feeling of happiness and freedom." I met Rainer when she came to accept an honorary award from the Motion Picture Academy and she told me that her most vivid memory of the apartment was explaining to her parents that she did not model for the Kolbe bronze nude that appears in Schulman's photo.

Soon after she left, the newly married Charles and Ray Eames lived and worked here until they moved to their iconic house in Pacific Palisades at Christmas 1949. They were workaholics who returned from their studio to continue their experiments in bending plywood. Ray hauled up massive timbers to construct the Kazam! a crude press, in which they baked their samples overnight. Regula Niedermann, Neutra's sister-in-law, who managed the apartments, called to ask why the electric bill was so huge, and why neighbors' lights were fluttering. Charles sternly rebuffed her: "It's war work; ask no questions." Indirectly it was, for they were mocking up the splint that was later mass-produced for the US Navy and would save the legs of countless wounded servicemen.

Homage to De Stijl

With advice from friendly professionals and the creativity of talented artisans, I've fleshed out the spaces as a tribute to the cool geometry of Neutra and the organic invention of the Eames. The goal was to foster a dialogue—enriched by personal memories and enthusiasms—between those giants, weaving together old and new, metal and wood, angles and curves. To avert cabin fever—I often spend entire days at a time in this 1,250-square-foot apartment when there's a book to be finished—I wanted each space to have a distinct character.

Here I must admit to a conflict. The part of me that admires the purity of the pioneers wishes I had left the space as I first found it; the part that craves beautiful objects—architect-designed furniture, vintage black and white photographs, limited-edition prints, and an abundance of books—recognizes the inevitability of layering the empty rooms and shielding them from the sun. Walking up from the street, I see the same facade that greeted Rainer and the Eameses. Within, everything has evolved. The living room and artworks are monochromatic. There's constant play of shadows from the plantings, and opening the levolor blinds in the morning turns the walls into a barred geometry of light and shade.

Neutra made little use of color (except for a bathroom tiled in iridescent blue), but other contemporaries—Le Corbusier and the De Stijl group in Holland—loved primary hues and my bedroom is a homage to them. Waking, I feel I'm in a golden cornfield with a clear, blue sky above and a comforting red glow at my back. The contrast with my celadon-walled office is exhilarating. And the contrasts make me forget how snug the apartment is. The kitchen is a narrow galley, but everything is close to hand. The architect's machine for living has been swallowed up by its garden, which blurs the crisp forms, as my possessions soften the interior lines.

Organic curves complement sharp angles in the living room

Treasures include a maquette that Frank Gehry reworked in resin, an early sketch by Zaha Hadid that suggests an explosion in outer space, a classic Cartier-Bresson image of a child in Valencia, and a Sebastião Salgado photograph of an iceberg to cool me down on hot days. There's a carved oak panel from an English Tudor house and a collage by Scott Johnson, Ruscha prints, and a watercolor of the Centrale Termica, the Futurist power station in Florence. The apartment has become an anthology of my passions that combines the shock of the new with the serenity former residents admired.

When I lose mobility and can no longer travel abroad, I shall have a domestic realm to explore in even greater detail. The wheel will have come full circle to that first, involuntary journey of my childhood. [2018]

Stilt walkers, Rome

Michael Webb was born and educated in London. He was an editor at The Times and Country Life, before relocating to Washington DC in 1969 as AFI Director of National Film Programming. The French Government named him Chevalier de l'Ordre des Arts et des Lettres for his services to French culture. In 1978, Michael moved to Los Angeles and left the AFI to write and consult on the arts. He curated Hollywood: Legend and Reality, the acclaimed Smithsonian exhibition, which toured to leading museums in the USA and Japan, wrote the companion book, and created film sequences within the exhibition. He also produced an Emmy-nominated television special, The Greatest Story Ever Sold.

Michael is the author of 28 books, most recently Architects' Houses, and Building Community: New Apartment Architecture. Previous titles include Modernist Paradise: Niemeyer House, Boyd Collection, Venice CA: Art +Architecture in a Maverick Community, Adventurous Wine Architecture, Art/ Invention/House, Through the Windows of Paris, Modernism Reborn: Mid-Century Modern American Houses, The City Square, and Hollywood: Legend and Reality. He has contributed essays to many other titles, as well as to travel and architectural journals in the US, Europe, and Asia.

ILLUSTRATIONS

All photographs were taken by the author, except for the image of *Fire Over London* from the Mary Evans/Grenville Collins Post Card Collection (p10); the poster for *An American in Paris*, MGM via All Posters (p11); the Ohio Theatre by D.F.Goff (p 44); the Gilardi House by Rebeca Mendez (p 82); and Marina One by H.G. Esch, courtesy of Gustafson Porter + Bowman (p 104). Back cover: The Churchill Arms pub on Kensington Church Street, London.

Goff Books
Published by Goff Books. An Imprint of ORO Editions
Gordon Goff: Publisher

www.goffbooks.com
info@goffbooks.com

Text by Michael Webb
Photography by Michael Webb unless otherwise specified
Book Design by Pablo Mandel / CircularStudio.com
Managing Editor: Jake Anderson

10 9 8 7 6 5 4 3 2 1 First Edition

ISBN: 978-1-940743-75-2

Color Separations and Printing: ORO Group Ltd.
Printed in China.

Goff Books makes a continuous effort to minimize the overall carbon
footprint of its publications. As part of this goal, ORO Editions, in
association with Global ReLeaf, arranges to plant trees to replace those used
in the manufacturing of the paper produced for its books. Global ReLeaf
is an international campaign run by American Forests, one of the world's
oldest nonprofit conservation organizations. Global ReLeaf is American
Forests' education and action program that helps individuals, organizations,
agencies, and corporations improve the local and global environment by
planting and caring for trees.